ANNO CHECKLIST OF THE BIRDS OF CUBA 2023

Number 6

Nils Navarro Pacheco

EDICIONES NUEVOS MUNDOS
The Friendship Association

www.EdicionesNuevosMundos.com

Senior Editor: Nils Navarro Pacheco

Editors: Soledad Pagliuca, Kathleen Hennessey and Sharyn Thompson

Corrections: Jeff Gerbracht

Cover Design: Scott Schiller

Cover: Cuban Sharp-shinned Hawk/Gavilancito Cubano (*Accipiter striatus fringilloides*), female, Parque Nacional Alejandro de Humboldt, Baracoa, Guantánamo, Cuba. Photo Nils Navarro, 2022

Back and front cover photo and Illustrations: ©Nils Navarro, 2022 and Nils Navarro, © *Endemic Birds of Cuba. A Comprehensive Field Guide*, 2015

Published by Ediciones Nuevos Mundos
www.EdicionesNuevosMundos.com
sole@edicionesnuevosmundos.com

ISBN: 9798847678254

Annotated Checklist of the Birds of Cuba

©Nils Navarro Pacheco, 2023

©Ediciones Nuevos Mundos, 2023

Recommended citation

Navarro, N. (2023). *Annotated Checklist of the Birds of Cuba, 2023*. Ediciones Nuevos Mundos, (6).

*To the memory of Jim Wiley, a great friend, extraordinary person and scientist, a guiding light of Caribbean ornithology.
He crossed many troubled waters in pursuit of expanding our knowledge of Cuban birds.*

About the Author

Nils Navarro Pacheco (1971) was born in Holguín, Cuba. He is a naturalist, author and an internationally acclaimed wildlife artist and scientific illustrator. A graduate of the Academy of Fine Arts with a major in painting, he served as curator of the herpetological collection of the Holguín Museum of Natural History, where he described several new species of lizards and frogs for Cuba.

Nils has been travelling throughout the Caribbean Islands and Middle America working on different projects related to the conservation of biodiversity, with a particular focus on birds, reptiles, and amphibians. He is the author of the book *Endemic Birds of Cuba, A Comprehensive Field Guide*, which, enriched by his own illustrations, creates a personalized field guide style that is both practical and useful, with icons as substitutes for texts adapted to local needs and interests. It also includes other important features based on his personal experience and understanding of the needs of field guide users. Nils continues to contribute his artwork and copyrights to BirdsCaribbean, other NGOs, and national and international institutions in an effort to help raise funds to support bird conservation in the Caribbean region.

Nils is currently **eBird** reviewer for Cuba, and author of the *Annotated Checklist of the Birds of Cuba* series, an annual publication that has become the official list of the birds of Cuba, which makes it the most up-to-date and complete reference on the subject throughout the territory, also he is cofounder of the "Cuban Big Year", which has become the most relevant action of citizen science on the country, improving the Cuban birdwatching movement. Currently he is working on a new *Comprehensive Field Guide to the Birds of Cuba*, as both the author and illustrator.

Foreword

The *Annotated Checklist of the Birds of Cuba* is an annual publication that grew from the need to provide updated information about changes that affect birds occuring in the Cuban archipelago. Development of new techniques in molecular studies, new interpretations of speciation and evolutionary phenomena have also emerged, considerably modifying the traditional way of viewing ornithology and resulting in rapid changes in taxonomy and systematics, often beyond what we can assimilate through the normal flow of information.

In addition, the growing demand for bird-watching tourism on the island and the implementation of monitoring programs of migratory species are contributing to an increase in the number of previously unrecorded species entering the list every year. Furthermore, the influence of climate change is producing altered patterns of migratory movements in many species.

Our main objective is to provide up-to-date annual listings of Cuban birds, including reference information on each new report and general statistics about Cuban birdlife, and to serve as a reference platform for ornithological studies in the country. It is our obligation to make this publication accessible to the community of local ornithologists and to the institutions involved in the conservation and study of Cuban birds.

This checklist is built on and optimized in each issue based on the needs and concerns of the local and regional ornithological community. We recommend keeping each edition, as every year, new important information appears, especially in the Comments section. Each list is considered valid for the corresponding year of publication. New additions and comments can be followed in "real time" through our Facebook page: www.facebook.com/groups/517785205380651. The PDF version is available for free; the printed version can be purchased through Amazon.com at a very accessible price. The minimal funds generated are used to support these annual publications.

Nils Navarro
Senior Editor

Contents

Contents 6
Acknowledgements 9
1.1. Before using the checklist 10
   1.2. Listed species 10
   1.3. Taxonomic sequence 11
   1.4. Species in conflict 12
   1.5. English name 12
   1.6. Common name 12
   1.7. Scientific name 13
      1.7.1. Subspecies 13
      1.7.2. Subspecies groups 13
      1.7.3. Status at specific level 14
   1.8. Alpha codes 14
   1.9. Conservation status 14
   1.10. Endemism and Endemic region 15
   1.11. Abundance status 15
   1.12. Breeding status 16
   1.13. Resident status 16
   1.14. Exotic and introduced species 17
   1.15. Distribution 18
1.16. General symbols 18
1.17. Unusual environmental events 18
1.18. New records and other additions 19
   1.19. About the new records and reports of rare birds 20
1.20. About the section "Comments" 21
1.21. About eBird 21
1.22. Useful links 21
1.23. Table 1: ANNOTATED CHECKLIST OF THE BIRDS OF CUBA (MAIN LIST) 23
1.24. DUCKS, GEESE AND SWANS 23
   Order: ANSERIFORMES   Family: Anatidae 23
1.25. QUAIL AND ALLIES 24
   Order: GALLIFORMES   Family: Numididae 24
   Order: GALLIFORMES   Family: Odontophoridae 24
   Order: GALLIFORMES   Family: Phasianidae 24
1.26. FLAMINGOS 24
   Order: PHOENICOPTERIFORMES Family: Phoenicopteridae 24
1.27. GREBES 24
   Order: PODICIPEDIFORMES   Family: Podicipedidae 24
1.28. DOVES AND PIGEONS 25
   Order: COLUMBIFORMES   Family: Columbidae 25
1.29. CUCKOOS AND ANIS 25
   Order: CUCULIFORMES   Family: Cuculidae 25
1.30. NIGHTHAWKS, NIGHTJARS AND POTOOS 26
   Order: CAPRIMULGIFORMES Family: Caprimulgidae 26
   Order: NYCTIBIIFORMES   Family: Nictibiidae 26
1.31. SWIFTS AND HUMMINGBIRDS 26
   Order: APODIFORMES Family: Apodidae 26
   Order: APODIFORMES   Family: Trochilidae 26

1.32. MARSH BIRDS 27
Order: GRUIFORMES   Family: Rallidae 27
Order: GRUIFORMES   Family: Aramidae 27
Order: GRUIFORMES   Family: Gruidae 27
Order: CHARADRIIFORMES Family: Recurvirostridae 27
Order: CHARADRIIFORMES Family: Haematopodidae 28
Order: CHARADRIIFORMES   Family: Charadriidae 28
Order: CHARADRIIFORMES   Family: Jacanidae 28
Order: CHARADRIIFORMES   Family: Scolopacidae 28

1.33. GULLLIKE BIRDS 29
Order: CHARADRIIFORMES   Family: Stercorariidae 29
Order: CHARADRIIFORMES   Family: Alcidae 30
Order: CHARADRIIFORMES   Family: Laridae 30
Order: PHAETHONTIFORMES Family: Phaethontidae 31
Order: GAVIIFORMES   Family: Gaviidae 31
Order: PROCELLARIIFORMES   Family: Oceanitidae 31
Order: PROCELLARIIFORMES Family: Hydrobatidae 31
Order: PROCELLARIIFORMES Family: Procellariidae 31
Order: CICONIIFORMES   Family: Ciconiidae 31
Order: SULIFORMES   Family: Fregatidae 32
Order: SULIFORMES   Family: Sulidae 32
Order: SULIFORMES   Family: Anhingidae 32
Order: SULIFORMES   Family: Phalacrocoracidae 32
Order: PELECANIFORMES   Family: Pelecanidae 32

1.34. HERONLIKE BIRDS 32
Order: PELECANIFORMES   Family: Ardeidae 32
Order: PELECANIFORMES Family: Threskiornithidae 33

1.35. HAWKLIKE BIRDS 33
Order: CATHARTIFORMES   Family: Cathartidae 33
Order: ACCIPITRIFORMES   Family: Pandionidae 33
Order: ACCIPITRIFORMES   Family: Accipitridae 33

1.36. OWLS 34
Order: STRIGIFORMES   Family: Tytonidae 34
Order: STRIGIFORMES   Family: Strigidae 34

1.37. TROGONS, TODIES AND ALLIES 35
Order: TROGONIFORMES   Family: Trogonidae 35
Order: CORACIIFORMES   Family: Todidae 35
Order: CORACIIFORMES   Family: Alcedinidae 35

1.38. WOODPECKERS 35
Order: PICIFORMES   Family: Picidae 35

1.39. FALCONS AND ALLIES 35
Order: FALCONIFORMES   Family: Falconidae 35

1.40. PARROTS AND PARAKEETS 36
Order: PSITTACIFORMES   Family: Psittacidae 36

1.41. FLYCATCHERS AND ALLIES 36
Order: PASSERIFORMES   Family: Tyrannidae 36

1.42. VIREOS AND CROWS 37
Order: PASSERIFORMES   Family: Vireonidae 37
Order: PASSERIFORMES   Family: Laniidae 38
Order: PASSERIFORMES   Family: Corvidae 38

1.43. SWALLOWS 38

Order: PASSERIFORMES   Family: Hirundinidae 38
1.44. KINGLETS, WAXWINGS, GNATCATCHERS AND WRENS 38
   Order: PASSERIFORMES   Family: Regulidae 38
   Order: PASSERIFORMES   Family: Bombycillidae 38
   Order: PASSERIFORMES   Family: Polioptilidae 39
   Order: PASSERIFORMES   Family: Troglodytidae 39
   Order: PASSERIFORMES   Family: Mimidae 39
   Order: PASSERIFORMES   Family: Sturnidae 39
1.45. SOLITAIRES, THRUSHES AND MIMICS 39
   Order: PASSERIFORMES   Family: Turdidae 39
1.46. FINCHES AND SPARROWS 40
   Order: PASSERIFORMES   Family: Estrildidae 40
   Order: PASSERIFORMES   Family: Muscicapidae 40
   Order: PASSERIFORMES   Family: Passeridae 40
   Order: PASSERIFORMES   Family: Motacillidae 40
   Order: PASSERIFORMES   Family: Fringillidae 40
   Order: PASSERIFORMES   Family: Calcariidae 40
   Order: PASSERIFORMES   Family: Passerellidae 40
1.47. SPINDALIS, BLACKBIRDS, ORIOLES AND ALLIES 41
   Order: PASSERIFORMES   Family: Spindalidae 41
   Order: PASSERIFORMES   Family: Teretistridae 41
   Order: PASSERIFORMES   Family: Icteriidae 41
   Order: PASSERIFORMES   Family: Icteridae 42
1.48. WARBLERS 42
   Order: PASSERIFORMES   Family: Parulidae 42
1.49. TANAGERS, GROSSBEAKS, BUNTINGS AND ALLIES 45
   Order: PASSERIFORMES   Family: Cardinalidae 45
   Order: PASSERIFORMES   Family: Thraupidae 45
1.50. Table 2: Cuban Endemisms according to categories 46
1.51. Table 3: Exotics and unsuccessful introduced species, uncertain origin records 48
1.52. Table 4: Unconfirmed Forms 51
1.53. Table 5: List of Fossil and Extinct Birds of Cuba* 52
1.54. Comments 54
1.55. List of additions and modifications at species and subspecies level in the main list subsequent to previous issues of the Checklist 65
1.56. Table 6: Cuban Birds, Numbers and Percentages 66
1.57. References 68

Acknowledgements

Each issue of this publication has been made possible thanks to the help of many friends, colleagues, institutions and NGOs.

To Orlando Garrido, Herbert Raffaele, Jim Wiley†, Marshall Iliff, Jeff Gerbracht, Andrea Holbrook, Natalia Rossi, for their contributions, ideas, time, support and accurate reviews. Thanks to "The Pamela and Alexander Skutch Research Award for Studies in Avian Natural History" of The Association of Field Ornithologists and the Mohamed Bin Zayed Conservation Fund; their support made it possible to increase the information related to Cuban avifauna, in particular with relation to Critically Endangered species. Special thanks to Javier Torres and Bárbara Sánchez (Baby) who helped create a databank of publications about Cuban birds.

Lisa Sorenson, Joni Ellis, Gary Markowski and Wally Van Sickle III, have been a decisive support to the successful production of each publication.

To BirdsCaribbean, Optics for the Tropics, Holbrook Travel, eBird Team, Ediciones Nuevos Mundos, Idea Wild, Mohamed Bin Zayed Conservation Fund, Caribbean Conservation Trust, Wildlife Conservation Society, Museum of Comparative Zoology (MCZ), Harvard University, The Peregrine Fund, Patuxent Wildlife Research Center, SalvaPC, APRM Este del Archipiélago de los Colorados for their encouragement and support.

To my friend Yaroddys Rodríguez (Yaro) who has been a part of this publication, for his excelent field experience, support, suggestions and friendship. His deep knowledge of Cuba´s ornithological history makes him in an irreplaceable source.

To my friend and colleague from eBird, Andy Mitchell, for his trust and unconditional support at all times, as well as for his insightful critiques of the manuscript.

To Scott Schiller who kindly created wonderful designs for the issues and dedicated much of his time working on it, my most sincere thanks!

My sincere thanks to (in alphabetical order): Ailen Anido, Alejandro Llanes, Alexeis Hernández, Alina Pérez, Angel Árias, Angel Abreu, Bárbara Sánchez, Carlos Hernández, Carlos Peña, Craig Robson, Denis LePage, Denny Swaby, Duniesky Urbano, Edelis Figueredo, Edwin Rojas, Elifaz E. Reyes, Elissa Landre, Ernesto Reyes, Feliberto Bermúdez (Felix)†, Felix Raúl Figueroa, Gerardo Hechavarría, Gerhard Aubrecht, Giraldo Alayón, Hiram González, Ianela García Lau, Ibalut Ruiz, Ivan Guerra, Jeremiah Trimble, Jorge Uría, Jose Luis Gómez, Juan Freile, Kate Eldridge, Karlos Ross, Kenia Medina, Laura Leyva, Luis Lajonchere, María Josefa Cordovés, Maikel Cañizares, Marvin and Lee Cook, Mohammad Halim Machado, Mirza Pérez, Noel Coutín, Norvis Hernández, Odey Martínez, Omar labrada, Orestes Martínez (El Chino Zapata), Orlando Marrero, Pedro Genaro, Rachel Greenwood, Rafael Rodríguez (Rafy), Robert Lockett, Robert Norton†, Roberto Jovel, Roberto Montero, Russell Thorstrom, Sergio López del Castillo, Terence Stephen Wright, Vanessa Claire, Vladimir Mirabal, Wildesnilde Navarro (El Indio de Humbolt), Yadier Molina, Yaquelín Rodríguez.

To Marlene Soto, curator of the Museum and collection of Charles T. Ramsden from Universidad de Oriente, for her dedication and support.

Rodolfo Castro (Fofito) for sharing his experience and field data from more than 12 years of monthly monitoring in the "Los Palacios" wetlands and to Johanset Orihuela for his comments and suggestions related to extinct fossil species.

To my great friend Patricia Lancho, who, from a distance, has been an essential support during all these years.

To the team at Ediciones Nuevos Mundos: Sole, Kate and Sharyn, with my eternal appreciation for their exceptional job and patience.

To my wife Yerenia, my sons Diego, Noel and Alejandro, my father (Nils) and mother (Magalys), brother (Alberto) and my little granddaughter Ashley (Susanita) thanks for allowing me to steal the time I should have dedicated to the family. To Ale and his office of his own SalvaPC for helping me with surveys around the eastern part of Cuba and for his technical support.

To the eBird community who, with their observations, contribute every day to broadening the knowledge of the birds in Cuba and around the world.

1.1. Before using the checklist

It is very important to read the following section carefully in order to understand each category. For example, to get a better understanding of the category "Abundance Status", it must be linked with each "Distribution Pattern". A species or subspecies that may look Uncommon on the island could appear as Fairly Common due to its distribution status: Local, Regional or Quasi-Cuban.

This publication is designed to be the official list of the birds of Cuba, supplying further background information to update every change related to ornithology in Cuba, and serving as a baseline of support to any ornithological study in the area of coverage. It is not intended to be a field guide or birding tour checklist.

I have followed some of the variables and criteria used by Gerbracht and Levesque (2019 and Gerbracht and Levesque draft) for the West Indies, and in some cases these were adjusted as necessary to local Cuban conditions.

I suggest using as complementary material the *"The Birds of Cuba, an Annotated Checklist"* (Kirkconnell et al., 2020), which provides a thorough review of each species. It is important to highlight that some criteria and points of view in the above-mentioned checklist differ from those assumed in this checklist, and, when significant, have been discussed in the present and former issues.

1.2. Listed species

Criteria for the forms (species or subspecies) listed here are as follow:

- **Undocumented Records**: all those that do not come from reliable sources, or if so, that do not include public credible supporting information: descriptions, specimens or their parts, photos, videos, recordings, etc. Records, including those published in scientific journals, whose descriptions and data do not provide clarity to the report are also considered. These records are treated in this publication within the list of Unconfirmed species.

- **Documented Records**: Until recently, documented records have been considered only those that have: specimen or its parts, photo, video, recording or other graphic or physical material. Additionally, a record, containing an accurate description of the bird will be considered as documented, as long as it meets certain requirements, so we have considered the evidence, taking into account the type of evidence available:

    From physical or graphic material: It has been the classic option for years, even the only valid one for many authors, sometimes disdaining other types of records, without case analysis, considering them as "Undocumented". This form includes: specimen, photos, videos, recordings or any other graphic material from a reliable source. These types of records meet the necessary requirements; have been considered valid and therefore are included in the main list.

    From an illustration or field notes: For various reasons, the observer made field notes, in color or black and white, which may be accompanied by some comment with the precise data or, at least, the basic. This note must incorporate the appropriate diagnostic characters to be considered valid. This reference does not necessarily always appear explicit as a new record in the original media. For example, the illustrations that Laudelino Bueno made in his diaries, in which he illustrated, sometimes without knowing it, several new species for Cuba that were brought to him for the zoo he managed. These types of records have been considered valid and are included in the main list.

    From a valid description: The least common and most controversial, so they require a casuistic analysis. Some authors do not consider valid any record that is not physically or graphically documented. Those records, when documented through a detailed description, published in a relevant specialized journal, whose authorship was made by a recognized expert in the field of ornithology, were considered valid. Observations involving two or more witnesses are more appropriate. In any case they should include a diagnostic "field characterization" of the bird, something that many new records do not include, simply mentioning that they were identified by someone or using a field guide or that the bird showed the typical characteristics of the species, etc., which adds a marked level of uncertainty. This usually applies to a species with a very characteristic diagnosis and where the bird could be observed in detail and for a reasonable time, which must be demonstrated through the text. In the case of groups whose diagnosis is complex (pewees, vireos, sparrows, shorebirds, etc.), a record of this type must be handled with caution.

In the current issue, the use of the term "**hypothetical forms**" (Table 3) is replaced by the term "**unconfirmed forms**". The term hypothetical can lead to confusion and does not really describe the idea of what is required to be shown.

We include references citations and comments (in superscripts) for the more recent or rare records, and when further important information is needed to clarify its status.

The basic terminology and concept of this checklist were adapted to local conditions from Gerbracht and Levesque (2019).

Improved alignment and consolidation of independent taxonomic studies are goals of the newly restructured International Ornithologists´ Union (IOU). List editors and interested colleagues participated in a vigorous round table discussion and follow-up at the August 2018 Congress in Vancouver, British Columbia. There was broad consensus and support for a global checklist of birds to serve as the standard reference for the class Aves. Consequently, a proposal was submitted to the IOU Executive Committee to form a Working Group on Global Avian Checklists, (https://www.internationalornithology.org/working-group-avian-checklists).

A new revision in 2022 begins the process of alignment of world checklists through the collaborative WGAC (Working Group Avian Checklists) process, which involves representatives from eBird/Clements, Avibase, AOS-NACC, AOS-SACC, the IOU World BirdList, BirdLife International, and other global experts in taxonomy, nomenclature, and classification. The effort is under the auspices of the IOU (International Ornithologists' Union) and is ongoing, with about 50% of the world's bird species assessed and an anticipated publication of a final, consensus world bird list in about two years.

I incorporate some of taxonomic decisions that represent consensus views of the WGAC, as a beginning on the process of aligning with this effort and supporting it in the future. On this issue they split Greater Antillean Nightjar into two species: Cuban (*Antrostomus cubanensis*) and Hispaniolan Nightjar (*A. ekmani*).

As we lack an international taxonomic consensus yet, this new edition has been updated with the latest taxonomic changes following the 63nd AOS Supplement (Chesser et al., 2022) and the WGAC-2022 (eBird, 2022).

This checklist also includes changes in sequences working at the subspecific level, whereas in the first issue (Navarro and Reyes, 2017) we listed only the species level. Some forms have been moved from the main list to the supplementary lists, and included in tables 2-5, but only the birds on the main list are considered to be a part of the Cuban birdlife. The new integrated concept makes this checklist more practical; the goal of the Comments section is to clarify incongruencies generated by the use of different taxonomic philosophies to record significant data among the world lists currently in use, and to update systematics, taxonomy, nomenclature and any other necessary comments.

1.3. Taxonomic sequence

The order in which taxa are sorted is based on the eBird/Clements Checklist v22 (Clements et al 2022) updated with the 63nd Supplement (Chesser et al., 2022) and WGAC-2022 (eBird, 2022). Sequences could vary depending on the taxonomic philosophy. Lists such as IOC World List; British Ornithological Union List, and The Howard & Moore Complete Checklist of the Birds of the World, 4th Edition follow other taxonomic criteria and sequence order.

Uniting the taxonomic treatments and philosophies from different regional authorities into a single, cohesive list is no small task. Inevitably, conflicts exist, both on specific issues and in general approaches to species limits, English names, scientific names, the sequence of species, genera, families, and other matters.

At the most fundamental level, we adhere to the Biological Species Concept (BSC), even for allopatric taxa in which the potential for interbreeding can only be inferred by the preponderance of evidence. For the Western Hemisphere, our first authority remains the American Ornithological Society (AOS), which has two committees that publish regular updates: the North American Classification Committee (NACC) covers the taxonomy and nomenclature of North American birds, publishes the official checklist of North American Birds (AOU), and publishes annual supplements to its own checklist in *The Auk*.

For South American birds, I follow the South American Classification Committee (SACC), which presents a scholarly treatment of all species occurring south of Panama. They post their findings (plus literature citations and clarifications), as decisions are made, on the SACC website. Usually these two committees agree with each other with regard to species that occur in both North and South America, but occasionally their taxonomies conflict. In such rare instances, I choose which taxonomy to follow depending on whether the affected species are primarily North or South American.

Some taxa and statuses are accepted that have not been officially recognized by the North American AOS committee, based on recognition by local authorities and publications in peer review journals, which demonstrate scientific support to split them.

For further comparisons among taxonomic lists in use, I suggest referring to the different Checklist versions at Avibase (https://avibase.bsc-eoc.org).

1.4. Species in conflict

Some taxa treated in this list have not been accepted by regional authorities such as AOS-NACC or eBird/Clement (under the last revision and update 2022), which is why they are not assigned Alpha Codes. However, they have been recognized by other international authorities based on highly regarded publications that demonstrate the validity of each one, so I have considered treating them as valid species. Such taxa are the following:

Cuban Bullfinch/Negrito/*Melopyrrha nigra*/CUBU= **Cuban Bullfinch**/Negrito/*Melopyrrha nigra*/**CUBU**; see Garrido et al. (2014).

This WGAC-2022 revision begins the process of alignment of world checklists through the collaborative WGAC (Working Group Avian Checklists) process, which involves representatives from eBird/Clements, Avibase, AOS-NACC, AOS-SACC, the IOU World BNirdList, BirdLife International, and other global experts in taxonomy, nomenclature, and classification. The effort is under the auspices of the IOU (International Ornithologists' Union) and is ongoing, with about 50% of the world's bird species assessed and anticipated publication of a final, consensus world bird list in about two years. I decided to incorporate a number of taxonomic decisions that represent consensus views of the WGAC, as they begin the process of aligning with this effort and supporting it in the future (eBird, 2022).

1.5. English name

The English common name for each species is the one defined by the most current version of eBird/Clements Checklist v2022 (Clements et al., 2022) and Chesser et al., (2022), which also follows the NACC policy on English names, which is stated in the Foreword to the 6th edition of the Checklist of North American Birds (1983), and is further elaborated by the AOU Committee, 2007.

1.6. Common name

The Cuban Common Name (CCN) is the one used more commonly throughout the country to refer to any specific bird, according to Garrido and Kirkconnell (2011). It is not always the same as the standardized names in Spanish used by SEO (Sociedad Española de Ornitología), BirdLife International or similar. The CCN is useful for communication within the country. There are also other *local names* that are not included in this checklist. Keep in mind that some CCN could vary in pronunciation; often the local people contract words such as Carpintero Jabado, which becomes Carpintero Jabao, or Rabudita, which becomes Rabuita.

In relation to the new combinations of common names in Cuba, for the recent additions to the list, priority will be given to the designations of names in use in Cuba. For example: for the inclusion of *Quiscalus mexicanus*, whose spanish standardized name according to SEO is "Zanate Mexicano". Since "Zanate", which is a náhualt word, is not understandable in Cuba, since it is given the name used on the island for the members of that genus (*Quiscalus*), is "Chichinguaco" and the designation which alludes to the geographical area, according to the standardized SEO name, in this way it would remain as "Chichinguaco Mexicano". In the same way, *Ictinia mississippiensis* standardized as "Milano", is a term not in use in Cuba. Instead, these birds are known as "Gavilán". To achieve a better understanding of their local practical use, I propose using the name "Gavilán del Mississippi".

When there is no local name for the group on the island, the most appropriate one will be selected from the Avibase list www.avibase.bsc-eoc.org/avibase.jsp, as the standardized SEO names (www.seo.org/nombres-de-las-aves-del-mundo-en-castellano/) are adjusted to the local language.

1.7. Scientific name

The scientific name for each bird is the one defined by the most current version of the Birds of the World (Billerman et al., 2022), following Clements et al. (2022). All have been updated with the latest changes in the 63nd AOS Supplement (Chesser et al., 2022).

1.7.1. Subspecies

The last edition of the AOU Checklist to include subspecies was published in 1957 (5th edition). For reasons of expediency, the Committee reluctantly excluded treatment of subspecies in both the 6th and 7th editions.

Subspecies reflect biological diversity and play an important role in catching the attention of evolutionary, behavioral, ecological, and conservation biologists. After careful study, an unknown number of subspecies likely will unmask cryptic biological species, or "species-in-the-making" that constitute a significant element of newly evolving biodiversity. On the other hand, an uncertain number of current subspecies apply to poorly differentiated populations and thus cannot be validated by rigorous modern techniques.

Although a complete revision of North American avian subspecies has not been done, I refer readers to Avibase and Birds of the World, for more up-to-date treatments of subspecies. The Birds of the World project is systematically revising subspecies accounts for all birds.

As major world bird lists differ slightly in their primary goals and taxonomic philosophy, I decided to follow:

- The American Ornithological Society's (AOS) Checklist, which is the official source on the taxonomy of birds found in North and Middle America, including adjacent islands (Chesser et al., 2022)
- The eBird/Clements Checklist v2022 (Clements et al., 2022) which combines all taxa from the Clements Checklist and all additional categories from the eBird taxonomy, with brief range descriptions for all taxa.

Those forms that include several subspecies are shown as follows:

- The name in "black ink" at the specific level (binominal) followed by its status. This is commonly used when studies refer to the specific level where it is not necessary to include subspecies, such as with certain ecological research.

- The Latin name, in gray ink, of every subspecies (trinominal) reported for Cuba with its own status. This is very important when the goal of the study is to determine a taxonomic issue, bird monitoring and baselines. The term "Probable" is used to refer to those supposed forms, which due to their distribution area and probabilities could be those found in Cuba.

1.7.2. Subspecies groups

In December 2009, version 6.5 of the eBird/Clements Checklist adopted the concept of a "group", which initially was developed by eBird. A "group" is a distinctive (field identifiable) subspecies or group of subspecies. Group is not a formal taxonomic unit, but often represents a potential future split (and so groups are a valuable taxonomic tool for the savvy birder). Birders that faithfully enter groups in eBird will be rewarded by automatic updates to their lists if and when splits occur.

Some groups are monotypic, that is, they involve only a single subspecies, whereas others are polytypic, with two or more subspecies. We admit that it sometimes is confusing to refer to a single subspecies as a "group". We now identify all groups as monotypic or polytypic. This allows the user to distinguish easily between the groups that contain multiple subspecies, and those groups that consist only of a single subspecies. The entries identified in the spreadsheet as "subspecies" and as "group (monotypic)" together comprise the entirety of subspecies on the list, whereas the polytypic groups are a secondary level between subspecies and species.

The tables show the different species or subspecies with the name of the group (in parenthesis) to which they belong. Note that the name of the group can be repeated in several subspecies if it is polytypic, that is, if composed of several races, of which several are found in Cuba.

1.7.3. Status at specific level

Some experts focus their investigations only on a specific level (names in black ink), like some ecological studies and the information on subspecies will not be of great practical use. Consequently, I decided to show those forms that include more than one subspecies (and their respective group) in Cuba, in gray ink, also specifying the status for each one.

In case the user does not know the subspecific status of his observation, he only has to mark the corresponding box in the line written in black type.

1.8. Alpha codes

Alphabetic ("alpha") codes are abbreviations of English (four letters) or scientific bird names (six letters) that are employed by ornithologists as shorthand. They allow quicker data entry than filling out the full English or scientific name of a species and they can also serve to cross-check other recorded names or numeric data.

This checklist uses four-letter (English Name) Alpha Codes in accordance with the 63nd AOS Supplement (Chesser et al., 2022) proposed for 2168 Bird Species (and 113 Non-Species Taxa) by Peter Pyle and David F. DeSante, based on The Institute for Bird Populations (IBP).

The U.S. Bird Banding Laboratory (BBL) has long used alpha codes in banding data, and these codes have become an integral part of large ornithological programs across the United States and Canada. Inconsistencies have occurred in the rules governing the alpha codes of the BBL with those of IBP.

Some species lack an Alpha Code (no code). While they may be recognized locally as a full species, they have not been approved through an AOS-NACC Supplement, or they are Old World birds.

The use of Codes for naming Non-Species Forms: The Institute for Bird Populations (IBP) has defined 113 names and codes for non-species forms, including subspecies, unidentified species, and unidentified subspecies, hybrids, intergrades, morphs, and intermediate-morphs. For the sake of consistency and because the identification of these forms provides valuable information, we maintain these forms in this list.

1.9. Conservation status

The international conservation status categories are presented according to BirdLife International as the official Red List Authority for birds for IUCN Red List Categories/BirdLife DataZone (until 2022) and the Birds of the World (2022). At the local level I follow González et al. (2012). When two abreviations appear separated by forward slash (/), the first corresponds to IUCN and the second to González et al. (2012) (in italics). Global threat statuses are indicated with a gray background.

For terms and definitions, Bird Life International has followed http://datazone.birdlife.org/species/spcredcat:

Extinct (Ex): A taxon is Extinct when there is no reasonable doubt that the last individual has died. A species is presumed extinct when exhaustive surveys in known and/or expected habitat, at appropriate times (diurnal, seasonal, annual), and throughout its historic range have failed to record an individual. Surveys should be over a time frame appropriate to the species' life history.

Critically Endangered (Possibly Extinct) CR (PE): This is not an official category of the IUCN Red List, but a tag applied by BirdLife (and under review by the IUCN Red List) to identify those Critically Endangered species (see definition below), that are likely to be extinct, but for which there is a small chance that they may still be extant, and hence they should not be listed as Extinct until local or unconfirmed reports have been discounted, and adequate surveys have failed to find any individuals (see below for further details).

Critically Endangered (CR): A taxon is Critically Endangered when the best available evidence (severe population decline, very small population, very small geographic area occupied, or if the calculated probability of extinction during the next 10 years is >50%) indicates that it is facing an extremely high risk of extinction in the wild.

Endangered (EN): A taxon is Endangered when the best available evidence (large population decline, small population, small geographic area occupied, or if the calculated probability of extinction during the next 20 years is >20%) indicates that it is considered to be facing a very high risk of extinction in the wild.

Vulnerable (VU): A taxon is Vulnerable when the best available evidence (large population decline, small population, small geographic area occupied, or if the calculated probability of extinction during the next 20 years is at least 10%) indicates that it is considered to be facing a high risk of extinction in the wild.

Near Threatened (NT): A taxon is Near Threatened when it has been evaluated against the criteria but does not qualify for Critically Endangered, Endangered or Vulnerable now, but is close to qualifying for or is likely to qualify for a threatened category in the near future.

Least Concern (LC): A taxon is Least Concern when it has been evaluated against the criteria and does not qualify for Critically Endangered, Endangered, Vulnerable or Near Threatened. Widespread and abundant species are included in this category.

It is important to point out that, according to IUCN (2019), only taxa with categories of Vulnerable (VU), Endangered (EN) and Critically Endangered (CR) are included as Threatened species. All other categories (except Data deficient and No Assessed) do not count as threatened but do count as at risk of extinction.

1.10. Endemism and Endemic region

Endemism by categories (family, genus, species, and subspecies) of Cuba are listed on the additional table subsequent to the main list (Table 2).

The endemic region is the most restrictive overarching region of endemism for each endemic species, i.e., a species that occurs in both the Greater and Lesser Antilles is considered a West Indian endemic, whereas a species that is endemic to Cuba and Hispaniola is considered a Greater Antillean endemic (Gerbracht and Levesque, 2019).

West Indies (WI): A form that is not restricted to a single region but is restricted to islands in the West Indies (also includes Swan Island in western Caribbean).

Greater Antilles (GA): A form that is restricted to islands in the Greater Antilles (Cuba, Jamaica, Cayman Islands, Hispaniola, Puerto Rico and Virgin Islands, the Anegada Passage being the border between Greater and Lesser Antilles).

Western Caribbean (WC): A form that also includes islands in the Western Caribbean, i.e., San Andrés, Providencia and Swan Island.

Cuba (CU): A form that is restricted to the Cuban archipelago.

Lucayan (LY): A form that also occurs on islands in the Lucayan Archipelago (Bahamas, Turks and Caicos).

+: Indicates that core area of distribution is limited to West Indies (*sensu stricto*), but isolated localities exist outside of that range.

1.11. Abundance status

These are relative concepts to measure bird observation frequency. In general, this checklist follows the ranges given by Raffaele et al. (1998), which focus on West Indian birds and is updated by recent criteria from Kirkconnell et al. (2020).

There is no complete study of the abundance of every Cuban bird species; consequently, there are gaps in this knowledge. In some cases, I have had to rely on historical records and information gathered from collections. I have also used the total number of sightings combined with the migratory source areas and estimated the real probability that a new sighting will occur. I focused on categories of rarity, splitting them into three: Rare (R), Very Rare (VR) and Exceptionally Rare (XR).

Common (Co): A form that occurs with high frequency. Five or more individuals likely to be seen daily in the appropiate habitat and season.

Fairly Common (FC): A form that occurs with moderate frequency. One to four individuals likely to be seen daily in the appropriate habitat and season.

Uncommon (U): A form that occurs with low frequency. Not likely to be seen on every expedition but can be seen at least twice per year.

Rare (R): Fewer than two records per year; expect at least one occurrence every five years, or more than three to 50 sightings in total.

Very Rare (VR): Occurs once every six to ten years, or those forms that had up to two sightings in total and came from traditional migrant sources such as North or South America, usually involving recognized migratory species (short distant migrants and non trans-oceanic).

Exceptionally Rare (XR): A form with only one sighting that occurs exceptionally. Usually, vagrant birds that do not come from traditional migratory source areas (Middle America, Old World or non-migratory species). Also applies to the special cases of Critically Endangered.

When there are two abundance statuses, for example: Co-R for a species, a hyphen (-) is used to indicate both statuses matching the column of residence status. If the status of abundance matches for both, it is only written once.

1.12. Breeding status

Breeding (Br): A form that reproduces within the Cuban archipelago.

Non-Breeding (-): A form that does not reproduce within the Cuban archipelago.

1.13. Resident status

The terms follow *The Birdwatcher's Dictionary*, Peter Weaver (1981) in the *Authoritative Dictionary of Birdwatching Terminology* (www.birdcare.com), adapted to similar terminologies currently in use in the region. The terms described below are applicable to the entire territory of the Cuban archipelago both on land and along its entire marine-platform and adjacent waters of the Cuban archipelago (especially in the case of pelagic species).

Year Round (YR): A form that is likely to occur throughout the entire year.

Partial Migrant (PM): Perhaps the most common type of bird migration in the world (Berthold, 2001, Jahn et al., 2006).

Partial migration is defined as a within-population variation in migratory behavior, meaning that some individuals migrate while others remain year-round residents in a given habitat. Studying a partially migratory population is the ideal system to test hypotheses concerning the evolution of migration and to elucidate costs and benefits of the two strategies (migration *versus* residency) (Zúñiga, 2016). A simpler concept explains partial migration as when a population of animals contains both migratory and resident individuals (Chapman et al., 2011).

The term partial migration derives predominantly from ornithological literature, where the phenomenon has long been recognized as being a common feature in the migration strategies of temperate-zone birds (Lack, 1943 and Newton, 2008).

It is important to distinguish between population-level partial migration and intra-population partial migration (Jahn et al., 2006):

1. **Population-level** partial migration: some populations of a species migrate and other populations do not. For example, in the case of the Broad-winged Hawk (*Buteo platypterus*) in Cuba, the nominate subspecies (*B. p. platypterus*) is a Nearctic migrant, while another subspecies (*Buteo p. cubanensis*) remains a permanent resident in the island.

2. **Intra-population level** partial migration: some individuals of the same population migrate after or before the breeding season and others do not. This is more frequent in shorebirds and other aquatic birds, as is the case of the American Avocet (*Recurvirostra americana*) in Cuba.

Superscript is used when the condition is potentially secondary, or indicates Partial Migratory (PM), winter (W) or summer (S) resident condition. The fact that part of a population remains in the archipelago all year round does not mean that it reproduces in these territories. Partial Migration is a strategy whereby many individuals not yet reproductively fit remain in the wintering territories.

In Cuba, the homologous local term "Bimodal Resident" was in use a few years ago (González, 1996; González et al., 2005; González et al., 2008; Ruiz et al., 2009; González and Pérez, 2010 and Rodríguez et al., 2014). However, I recommend applying the term Partial Migrant, as it has a more widespread use and is supported by in-depth research at the international level (Lundberg, 1988; Jahn et al., 2006; Chapman et al., 2011; Hegemann et al., 2015; Zúñiga, 2016 and Chambon et al., 2019), promoting the standardization of the terminology in use and increasing the visibility of articles in internet search engines.

Summer Resident (SR): A bird which uses a particular area for breeding only, therefore is absent outside the breeding season (breeding visitor). In Cuba, birds usually arrive from South America (mainly February/April to September/October); early migrants such as the Cuban Martin start arriving late January. Indicated in superscript^S when the condition is potentially secondary. Summer Residents are also called "Summer Visitors".

Winter Resident (WR): A bird that visits a particular area only for the winter and does not breed there (non-breeding visitor). As the Cuban archipelago has a tropical climate year-round, it hosts many WR from North America (mainly September/October to March/April) but early migrants could arrive in July or leave late in May). Indicated in superscript^W when the condition is potentially secondary. Winter Residents are also called "Winter Visitors".

Transient (T): Movement through an area involving individuals who neither breed nor spend the winter in Cuba, merely passing through on migration. As the Cuban archipelago lies on a major flyway, very large numbers of transients pass through each fall and spring (mainly September–October and April–May). Transients are also called "Passage Migrants".

Vagrant (V): A bird that wanders to a particular area if its orientation is at fault or adverse winds drive it off course, but under normal circumstances would not be found in Cuba. Vagrants are also called "accidentals" or "casuals".

Note: Many species have different timings of migration and the actual month ranges for these seasonality values will be different among species.

When there are two residence statuses, for example: T-WR for a species, a hyphen (-) is also used to indicate both abundance statuses: Co-R in the same sequence in which they appear in the first reference, if the status of abundance matches for both, it is only written once. The sequence in which each one appears on the table is as follow: V, T, WR, SR, PM, YR.

1.14. Exotic and introduced species

I adopt the definition of exotic species established in the Convention on Biological Diversity, which was proposed by the IUCN Group of Experts on Invasive Species (ISSG) (appendix to resolution VI/23, IUCN [2000]):

Exotic species: refers to species, subspecies or lower taxon, introduced outside their natural distribution in the past or present; this includes any parts, gametes, seeds, eggs or propagules of such species that could survive and subsequently reproduce.

It is considered as an "introduction" to the movement, by human action, indirect or direct, of an exotic species outside its natural environment (past or present). This movement can be carried out within a country or between countries or areas outside of the species´ national or geographic jurisdiction:

a) **Intentional introduction**: refers to the deliberate movement and/or release by humans of an exotic species outside of its natural environment.

b) **unintentional introduction**: refers to other types of introductions that are not intentional.

This checklist also combines the general categories that will be applied by eBird to exotic species (eBird, 2021), with the sub-categories used by the British Ornithologist Union set of definitions for introduced (exotic) species (www.bou.org.uk), adapted to Cuban conditions. This combination allows achieving greater definition in terms of certain specificities found in the Cuban avifauna. Sub-category C7 was created taking into consideration that the previous ones did not correspond to the condition of exotic species that became hybrids in the wild (Navarro, 2020):

1.14.1. Naturalized: (N)

Exotic population is self-sustaining, breeding in the wild, persisting for many years, and not maintained through ongoing releases (including vagrants from naturalized populations). These count in official eBird totals and, where applicable, have been accepted by regional bird records committee(s):

(C1): *Introduced species*– species that occur only as a result of introduction and for its reproduction depend absolutely on human support. They are not self-sustaining, living mainly in anthropic conditions. Exceptionally, they could locally reproduce in feral conditions in very low and isolated numbers, having no connectivity with others.

(C2): *Naturalized established species*– species with established populations in the wild resulting from introduction by humans, but which also occur in an apparently natural state.

(C3): *Naturalized re-established species*– species with populations successfully re-established by humans in areas of former occurrence.

(C4): *Naturalized feral species*– domesticated species with populations established in the wild.

(C5): *Vagrant naturalized species from foreign naturalized populations*– species from established naturalized populations abroad.

1.14.2. Provisional: (Pr)

Member of an exotic population that is breeding in the wild, self-propagating, and has persisted for multiple years, but not yet Naturalized; 2) rarity of uncertain provenance, with natural vagrancy or captive provenance both considered plausible. When applicable, eBird generally defers to bird records committees for records formally considered to be of «uncertain provenance». Provisional species count in official eBird totals:

(C6): *Former naturalized species* – species formerly placed in C1-5 whose naturalized populations are either no longer self-sustaining or are considered extirpated.

(C7): *Former naturalized species become hybrids* (new category [Navarro, 2020]) – species formerly placed in C1 whose naturalized populations, usually in small numbers, are prone to disappear due to the hybridization process.

Escapee: (E)

Exotic species known or suspected to be escaped or released, including those that have bred in the wild but don't yet fulfill the criteria for Provisional. Escapee exotics do not count in official eBird totals.

1.15. Distribution

Pan-Cuban (PC): widespread throughout the archipelago in the appropriate habitat and season.

Quasi-Cuban (QC): with a wide distribution in the appropriate habitat and season, but absent from part(s) of the country.

Regional distribution (Rg): Forms are restricted to a particular region: Eastern, Central or Western Cuba, e.g., the Yellow-headed Warbler lives only in western Cuba.

Local (L): Forms with very limited distribution mainly restricted to one or few sites, e.g., Zapata Wren in Zapata Swamp.

Point (P): Forms recorded in very few sites (specific geographic points), usually sightings of vagrant birds.

Open Waters (OW) (new term): Pelagic and marine forms living on the ocean that rarely visit coasts or inland but could be quite common in open waters surrounding Cuba. Sometimes they will appear combined with Points **(P)** as some records from coastal areas have described. Eventually those species could reach coasts or inland during severe weather disturbances.

1.16. General symbols

Uncertain status for any category is designated by a question mark (?).

1.17. Unusual environmental events

The cyclonic season coincides with the most important migratory processes that affect our archipelago, and knowing that these processes promote and enhance the arrival of rare species out of context, I considered it useful and necessary to make a summary of how the season developed in the previous year. The influences will appear during the winter residence for the year corresponding to each Checklist.

The annual summary is based on statistics provided by NOAA:

(https://www.nhcnoaa.gov/archive/tws/)

During the 2022 season, two phenomena affected Cuba. Alex constituted the first event as a tropical storm at the beginning of the season (June 5-6), which developed from the remnants of Tropical Storm Agatha in the Pacific, which when crossing Mexico became Tropical Depression Alex. This affected Cuba with rains and strong winds reaching 110 km/h in western Cuba. Consecuently, the first record of the Great-tailed Grackle (*Quiscalus mexicanus*) was detected in Havana. The second event that impacted Cuba was

Hurricane Ian, a major category 3 storm that hit the west of the island on September 27, causing enormous devastation, with winds of up to 250 km/h. Days later, abnormal numbers of Western Spindalis (Cuban) (*Spindalis zena pretrei*) were recorded in areas where they were never frequent, such as Havana city and surroundings, including a record in the Monroe County, Florida (see Comments). Records of Red-legged Honeycreeper were also produced in Florida and Louisiana (see Comments), which in my opinion is the result of the devastating impact on the vegetation of western Cuba, as well as the persistence of the large eye and storm cone generated by Ian during its passage over the mainland.

Given the high probability of the exchange of bird species between islands generated by the influence of extreme synoptic events such as hurricanes or cold fronts, it would be of great importance to implement monitoring plans focused on potential areas for this exchange after the passage of these events. I identified four fundamental areas of possible influence:

1. *Cabo de San Antonio*: area of influence for Central American and North American species.
2. *Cayería norte de Cuba*: area of influence for species from the Bahamas and rarities from North America.
3. *Punta de Maisí*: area of influence for Hispaniola species.
4. *Southern coast of Santiago de Cuba-Guantánamo*: area of influence for species from Jamaica.

1.18. New records and other additions

Despite the current limitations in Cuba, the still fledgling local community of Cuban bird watchers remained very active during 2022, participating in the greatest citizen science event in the history of Cuba, the "Cuban Big Year". Some new records resulted from of reviewing historical documents and birds captured by local "bird trappers" and incidental observations:

I. **Brant** (*Branta bernicla nigricans*): Observed and photographed in the Salinas, Ciénaga de Zapata, Matanzas, Cuba, by a group of birdwatchers. Record uploaded to eBird by Craig Robson and Robert Lockett (Robson, 2022 and Lockett, 2022). The bird was discovered and identified by Cynthia Lawes and the photos belong to Craig Robson and Alejandro Alfonso García (see section **1.54 Comments**).

II. **African Collared Dove** (*Streptopelia roseogrisea*): Guerra (2022) recorded this species in the city of Holguín, based on photos, videos and recordings of the song. The bird was next to a group of Eurasian Collared Doves in the neighborhood and was courting with them. It is very likely that it was an escaped bird from captivity since it was the domestic form (Guerra 2022).

III. **Pileated Woodpeaker** (*Dryocupus pileatus*): The record was made by Duniesky Urbano, fishing guide in Marina Marlin Jardines del Rey, in Sabana-Camaguey archipelago (Coco, Paredón, Guillermo). The bird was detected in the coastal area of Los Pinos beach. Duniesky showed the photo taken with a cell phone to another colleague, Yadier Molina Polo, who sent it to me for identification. Then the colleague Odey Martínez from the Flora and Fauna office directly contacted Duniesky who also provided him with the metadata information of the original image. He observed the bird for two days and commented that at first it was not shy but then it behaved very elusively, and he could only take pictures of it, for which he used the phone's zoom, on the first occasion, while the bird was foraging along a trunk of Uva Caleta (*Coccoloba uvifera*) (RARC, 2022a) in an area almost devoid of tree vegetation. Exiff data extracted from the original file: Galaxy S7 edge. 11 de febrero 8:28 AM. OMG 20220211-WA 0007.JPG. Resolución: 486x1080.

IV. **White-winged Becard** (*Pachyramphus polychopterus spp.*). Historical Records 1987, in a letter dated June 7, 1987 from Orlando Garrido to James Bond and accompanying detailed description, taken from personal files courtesy of Orlando H. Garrido. The partially decomposed body of the bird was found by Arturo Kirkconnell and James Edwardson (precise data in the attached text). It is interesting that this record had never been mentioned by any of the authors, not even by James Bond himself, possibly because this letter was written two years before his death in 1989. The origin of this specimen is uncertain and could be related to a "ship assisted" event.

V. **Shrike sp.** (probably **Loggerhead**) (*Lanius* (prob. *ludovicianus*): Illustrated in one of the diaries of Laudelino Bueno† (Historical Records 1985), who was director of the Cárdenas Zoo, Matanzas; in the illustration its author added the note: "Northern Shrike ave rara dono Julio Vasque" (sic).

The illustration was made with outline using pen and ink, apparently because it was a bird whose color varies between white, gray and black, and apparently he did not pay much attention to including chiaroscuro, however, the illustration is well diagnosable and its author emphasized characters such as: the structure of the bird, a black mask on the face, proportionally short bill, black wings and a white border on the tail, which were very explicit in the drawing. Although the author identifies it as a Northern Shrike (*Lanius excubitor*), it is very likely that it was the Loggerhead Shrike (*Lanius ludovicianus*), whose distribution even reaches Florida and also has been recorded as vagrant in Bahamas (Andros, Gran Bahama and Great Exuma) (Kirwan et al., 2019), the existence of a short beak and absence of bars on the chest, suggest that it could pertain to Loggerhead instead of Northern which has a barred breast, and not the one indicated by Laudelino in his diary. The bird was donated to Laudelino by Julio Vázquez, a local who trapped it, presumably in Cardenas, Matanzas.

VI. **Bohemian Waxwing** (*Bombicilla garrulus*): In one of Laudelino Bueno†'s diaries, he illustrates and includes a comment, among other topics, on Thursday, March 26, 1970: "I bring the picotero..." and then includes a fully diagnostic illustration of the species (Historical Records 1987). It is possible to appreciate the diagnostic characters that identify this species and differentiate it from Cedar Waxwing (B. cedrorum): uniform brownish-grey underparts (vs bicolor brown and yellow), lower tail coverts tan (vs white) and yellow wing lines (absent in *B. cedrorum*).

VII. **Song Sparrow** (*Melospiza melodia*): This individual was captured in the north Yara, Granma province (RARC, 2021) and held captive by a local birder, who uploaded the photo to social media to inquire about his identification.

VIII. **Great-tailed Grackle** (*Quiscalus mexicanus*): An individual of this species was observed for several weeks in Quinta de los Molinos, Havana, recorded for the first time by Muhammad Halim Machado (Halim, 2022). This individual apparently arrived in Cuba as a result of Hurricane Agatha passing through Mexico at the end of May, which when crossing, its remnants would in turn become the first cyclonic disturbance in the Atlantic in 2022 (June 2), designated as a tropical storm on June 5 and called "Alex". It hit western Cuba with heavy rains and coastal flooding from Yucatan, where hurricane-force winds and areas of intense rains could move birds from Central America.

1.19. About the new records and reports of rare birds

These rules must apply for the publication of new records or when dealing with species considered rare or very rare. They have the objective of guaranteeing the validity of said publication and avoiding reports whose identification may be questionable.

1. Include, whenever possible, graphic documentation, whether photos (of individuals, specimens), illustrations, videos or sonograms. Check that these show the diagnostic characters that identify the species. If it is a collection specimen, it is necessary to add the original data and catalog number with the proper acronym of the institution where it is deposited, and if it is a ringed bird, include the corresponding ring number. If the magazine or section does not allow the publication of photos, then I suggest that the record must be previously uploaded to the eBird platform and duly referenced (graphic documentation included): https://science.ebird.org/en/use-ebird-data/citation

2. When it is not possible to have the previous documentation, then a description must be included, as detailed as possible about the individual/specimen, which necessarily explains the diagnostic characters that allowed it to be differentiated from other similar species with which it could be confused.

3. Include as much anecdotal data and comments related to the registry as possible.

1.20. About the section "Comments"

IMPORTANT! This section contains numerical links to the content in the tables; the main objective is to update status changes and clarify uncertain situations or inconsistencies with other international lists in use.

Although each number of the checklist is valid for the corresponding year in terms of the species list, the comments are unique for each edition and can therefore affect subsequent publications.

Each new number of this Checklist is valid for the corresponding year; each of the important events related to new records, taxonomic changes and other topics of interest.

1.21. About eBird

eBird is an online database of bird observations that provides scientists, researchers and amateur naturalists with real-time data about bird distribution and abundance. Originally restricted to sightings from the Western Hemisphere, by 2010 it covered the whole world. eBird has been described as an ambitious example of enlisting amateurs to gather data on biodiversity for use in science that has become an incredibly useful tool.

eBird is an example of crowdsourcing, and has been hailed for democratizing science, treating citizens as scientists, allowing the public to access and use their own data and the collective data generated by others.

eBird's goal is to maximize the utility and accessibility of the vast numbers of bird observations made each year by recreational and professional bird watchers. The observations of each participant join those of others in an international network. Due to the variability in the observations the volunteers make, local eBird reviewers filter observations through collected historical data to improve accuracy. The data are then available via internet queries in a variety of formats.

Some tips to get better results uploading your list to eBird:

- Be sure that the sightings are well identified and placed in the right location. If the species is difficult to identify, look for help from an expert in the group.
- **VERY IMPORTANT!** Close the list when you finish one site and continue to another location. In Cuba completely different habitats are located very close to one another and a few meters or kilometres in between will count!
- When you use a mobile phone be sure to make the right selection of the species on the list; sometimes fingers unintentionally flag the next or previous species on the list.
- In the case of flagged species please add comments that explain the field marks used in the ID. The eBird reviewers will appreciate it, and a clear ID will help in the validation process of the sighting.
- When possible, add photos, videos, and audio recordings of the bird you are registering, especially with species flagged as Rare for the area. We recommend you upload every photo in the moment you submit the list.
- When recording species in high counts (+100) in addition to writing the number in the corresponding box, include the number again in Comments, also adding if the count is an "exact count" or by estimation, so that the reviewers can distinguish typo errors.
- New records of species for Cuba must be supported by graphic information such as photos, videos, or any kind of proof that supports the validity of the sighting.
- Now you can use the eBird "Subespecies Groups", when you are completely sure the bird you saw belongs to the right subspecies (group), if not, just use the Standard English Name.

This checklist is eBird friendly; it integrates the eBird names and forms making it easier for the eBird user to upload the data.

1.22. Useful links

eBird (upload your birdlist and explore): https://ebird.org/explore

Avibase (bird data, international checklists and taxonomy)
https://avibase.bsc-eoc.org/avibase.jsp?lang=EN

All About Birds (ID and sounds):
https://www.allaboutbirds.org/news/

Birds of the World (membership required):
https://birdsoftheworld.org/bow/home

Xeno-canto (bird calls database):
https://www.xeno-canto.org/

1.23. Table 1: ANNOTATED CHECKLIST OF THE BIRDS OF CUBA (MAIN LIST)

** species flagged with double asterisk were accepted under "Documented records" by a "valid description", and were made by experts, but lacking photos or other graphic material.

	English Name/Cuban Common Name (CCN)/*Latin Name*/Alpha Code	Threat status	End. Reg.	Abun. status	Breed status	Resid. status	Ext.	Dist.
	**1.24. DUCKS, GEESE AND SWANS**								
	**Order: ANSERIFORMES Family: Anatidae**								
1.	☐ *Dendrocygna viduata*/**White-faced Whistling-Duck**/Yaguasa Cariblanca/ **WFWD**	LC	-	R	-	V	-	P
2.	☐ *Dendrocygna autumnalis fulgens*/**Black-bellied Whistling-Duck (fulgens)**/Yaguasa Barriguiprieta/ **BBWD**	LC	-	R	?	YR[PM?]	-	P
3.	☐ *Dendrocygna arborea*/**West Indian Whistling-Duck**/Yaguasa Cubana/**WIWD**	NT	WI	FC	Br	YR	-	PC
4.	☐ *Dendrocygna bicolor*/**Fulvous Whistling-Duck**/Yaguasín/**FUWD**	LC	-	FC	Br	PM[W]	-	PC
5.	☐ *Anser caerulescens caerulescens*/**Snow Goose**/Guanana Prieta/**SNGO**	LC	-	R	-	V-T?-WR?	-	P
6.	☐ *Anser albifrons gambelli*/**Greater White-fronted Goose (Western)**/Guanana/**GWFG**	LC	-	R	-	V-T?-WR?	-	P
7.	☐ *Branta bernicla nigricans*/**Brant (Black)**/Ganso Carinegro/**BLBR**[1]	LC	-	VR	-	V	-	P
8.	☐ *Branta canadensis canadensis*/**Canada Goose (canadensis Group)**/Ganso de Canadá/**CANG**	LC	-	VR	-	V	-	P
9.	☐ *Cygnus columbianus* (prob. *columbianus*)/**Tundra Swan (Whistling)**/Cisne de la Tundra/**TUSW**	LC	-	VR	-	V	-	P
10.	☐ *Cairina moschata*/**Muscovy Duck (Established Feral)**/Pato Doméstico/**MUDU**	LC	-	U	Br	YR	**N-C4**	PC
11.	☐ *Aix sponsa*/**Wood Duck**/ Pato Huyuyo/**WODU**	LC	-	FC	Br	PM[W]	-	PC
12.	☐ *Spatula discors*/**Blue-winged Teal**/Pato de la Florida/**BWTE**	LC	-	Co	?	T-WR (PM?)	-	PC
13.	☐ *Spatula cyanoptera septentrionalium*/**Cinnamon Teal**/Pato Canelo/**CITE**	LC	-	R	-	V	-	P
14.	☐ *Spatula clypeata*/**Northern Shoveler**/Pato Cuchareta/**NSHO**	LC	-	Co	-	T-WR	-	PC
15.	☐ *Mareca strepera strepera*/**Gadwall (Common)**/Pato Gris/**GADW**	LC	-	R	-	WR	-	P
16.	☐ **Mareca penelope/**Eurasian Wigeon**/Pato Lavanco Eurasiático[2]/**EUWI**	LC	-	VR	-	V	-	P
17.	☐ *Mareca americana*/**American Wigeon**/Pato Lavanco/**AMWI**	LC	-	FC	-	T-WR	-	PC
18.	☐ *Anas platyrhynchos platyrhynchos*/**Mallard**/Pato Inglés/**MALL**	LC	-	R	-	T-WR	-	P
19.	☐ *Anas bahamensis bahamensis*/**White-cheeked Pintail (White-cheeked)**/Pato de Bahamas/**WCHP**	LC	-	FC	Br	YR	-	PC

	English Name/Cuban Common Name (CCN)/*Latin Name*/Alpha Code	Threat status	End. Reg.	Abun. status	Breed status	Resid. status	Ext.	Dist.
20.	☐ *Anas acuta*/**Northern Pintail**/Pato Pescuecilargo/**NOPI**	LC	-	U	-	T-WR	-	PC
21.	☐ *Anas crecca carolinensis*/**Green-winged Teal (American)**/Pato Serrano/**AGWT**	LC	-	FC	-	T-WR	-	PC
22.	☐ *Aythya valisineria*/**Canvasback**/Pato Lomiblanco/**CANV**	LC	-	R	-	WR	-	P
23.	☐ *Aythya americana*/**Redhead**/Pato Cabecirrojo/**REDH**	LC	-	R	-	V-T?	-	P
24.	☐ *Aythya collaris*/**Ring-necked Duck**/Pato Cabezón/**RNDU**	LC	-	Co	-	T-WR	-	PC
25.	☐ *Aythya affinis*/**Lesser Scaup**/Pato Morisco/**LESC**	LC	-	Co	-	T-WR	-	PC
26.	☐ *Melanitta perspicillata*/**Surf Scoter**/Negrón Careto (SEO)/**SUSC**	LC	-	VR	-	V	-	P
27.	☐ ***Melanitta deglandi*/**White-winged Scoter**/Negrón Especulado (SEO)/**WWSC**	LC	-	VR	-	V	-	P
28.	☐ *Bucephala albeola*/**Bufflehead**/Pato Moñudo/**BUFF**	LC	-	R	-	V	-	P
29.	☐ *Lophodytes cucullatus*/**Hooded Merganser**/Pato de Cresta/**HOME**	LC	-	R	-	T-WR	-	P
30.	☐ ***Mergus merganser* prob. *americanus*/**Common Merganser (North American)**/Pato Serrucho Raro/**COME**	LC	-	VR	-	V	-	P
31.	☐ *Mergus serrator*/**Red-breasted Merganser**/Pato Serrucho/**RBME**	LC	-	FC	-	T-WR	-	L
32.	☐ *Nomonyx dominicus*/**Masked Duck**/Pato Agostero/**MADU**	LC/*VU*	-	U	Br	YR	-	PC
33.	☐ *Oxyura jamaicensis*/**Ruddy Duck**/Pato Chorizo/**RUDU**	LC	-	FC	Br	PM^W	-	PC
1.25. QUAIL AND ALLIES								
Order: GALLIFORMES Family: Numididae								
34.	☐ *Numida meleagris galeatus*/**Helmeted Guineafowl (West African)**/Gallina de Guinea/**HELG**	LC	-	FC	Br	YR	**N-C4**	PC
Order: GALLIFORMES Family: Odontophoridae								
35.	☐ *Colinus virginianus cubanensis*/**Northern Bobwhite (Eastern)**/Codorniz/**NOBO**	NT	CU	FC	Br	YR	?	PC
Order: GALLIFORMES Family: Phasianidae								
36.	☐ *Phasianus colchicus* (prob. *torquatus*)/**Ring-necked Pheasant (Ring-necked)**/Faisán/**RNEP**	LC	-	U	Br	YR	**N-C1**	L
1.26. FLAMINGOS								
Order: PHOENICOPTERIFORMES Family: Phoenicopteridae								
37.	☐ *Phoenicopterus ruber*/**American Flamingo**/Flamenco/**AMFL**	LC	-	Co	Br	PM	-	QC
1.27. GREBES								
Order: PODICIPEDIFORMES Family: Podicipedidae								
38.	☐ *Tachybaptus dominicus dominicus*/**Least Grebe**/Zaramagullón Chico/**LEGR**	LC	-	Co	Br	YR	-	PC

	English Name/Cuban Common Name (CCN)/*Latin Name*/Alpha Code	Threat status	End. Reg.	Abun. status	Breed status	Resid. status	Ext.	Dist.
39.	☐ *Podilymbus podiceps*/**Pied-billed Grebe**/Zaramagullón Grande/**PBGR**	LC	-	Co	Br	PM[W]	-	PC
	☐ *Podilymbus podiceps podiceps*	LC	-	VR?	-	WR	-	P
	☐ *Podilymbus podiceps antillarum*	LC	WI	Co	Br	YR	-	PC

1.28. DOVES AND PIGEONS
Order: COLUMBIFORMES   Family: Columbidae

40.	☐ *Columba livia*/**Rock Pigeon (Feral Pigeon)**/Paloma Doméstica/**ROPI**	LC	-	Co	Br	YR	N-C4	PC
41.	☐ *Patagioenas squamosa*/**Scaly-naped Pigeon**/Torcaza Cuellimorada/**SNPI**	LC	WI+	FC	Br	YR	-	PC
42.	☐ *Patagioenas leucocephala*/**White-crowned Pigeon**/Torcaza Cabeciblanca/**WCPI**	NT/VU	-	Co	Br	PM	-	PC
43.	☐ *Patagioenas inornata inornata*/**Plain Pigeon**/Torcaza Boba/**PLAP**	NT/VU	GA	U	Br	YR	-	L
44.	☐ *Streptopelia decaocto decaocto*/**Eurasian Collared-Dove (Eurasian)**/Tórtola de Collar/**EUCD**[3]	LC	-	Co	Br	YR	N-C5	PC
45.	☐ *Ectopistes migratorius*/**Passenger Pigeon**/Paloma Migratoria/**PAPI**	Ex	-	-	-	-	-	-
46.	☐ *Columbina passerina insularis*/**Common Ground Dove**/Tojosa/**CGDO**	LC	GA	Co	Br	YR	-	PC
47.	☐ *Starnoenas cyanocephala*/**Blue-headed Quail-Dove**/Paloma Perdiz/**BHQD**	EN	CU	U	Br	YR	-	QC
48.	☐ *Geotrygon montana montana*/**Ruddy Quail-Dove (Ruddy)**/Boyero/**RUQD**	LC	-	FC	Br	YR	-	PC
49.	☐ *Geotrygon caniceps*/**Gray-fronted Quail-Dove**/Camao/**GFQD**	VU	CU	U	Br	YR	-	QC-L
50.	☐ *Geotrygon chrysia*/**Key West Quail-Dove**/Barbiquejo/**KWQD**	LC	-	FC	Br	YR	-	PC
51.	☐ *Zenaida asiatica asiatica*/**White-winged Dove**/Paloma Aliblanca/**WWDO**	LC	-	Co	Br	YR	-	PC
52.	☐ *Zenaida aurita zenaida*/**Zenaida Dove**/Guanaro/**ZEND**	LC	GA	Co	Br	YR	-	PC
53.	☐ *Zenaida macroura*/**Mourning Dove**/Paloma Rabiche/**MODO**	LC	-	Co	Br	PM[W]	-	PC
	☐ *Zenaida macroura macroura*	LC	GA	Co	Br	YR	-	PC
	☐ *Zenaida macroura carolinensis*[4]	LC	-	FC	-	WR	-	PC

1.29. CUCKOOS AND ANIS
Order: CUCULIFORMES   Family: Cuculidae

54.	☐ *Crotophaga ani*/**Smooth-billed Ani**/Judío/**SBAN**	LC	-	Co	Br	YR	-	PC
55.	☐ *Coccyzus americanus*/**Yellow-billed Cuckoo**/Primavera/**YBCU**	LC	-	FC	Br	T-SR	-	PC
56.	☐ *Coccyzus minor*/**Mangrove Cuckoo**/Arrierito/**MACU**	LC	-	U	Br	YR	-	PC

25

	English Name/Cuban Common Name (CCN)/*Latin Name*/Alpha Code	Threat status	End. Reg.	Abun. status	Breed status	Resid. status	Ext.	Dist.
57.	☐ *Coccyzus erythropthalmus*/**Black-billed Cuckoo**/Primavera de Pico Negro/**BBCU**	LC	-	R	-	T	-	P
58.	☐ *Coccyzus merlini*/**Great Lizard-Cuckoo (Cuban)**/Arriero o Guacaica/**GRLC**	LC	CU-LY	Co	Br	YR	-	PC
	☐ *Coccyzus merlini merlini*	LC	CU	Co	Br	YR	-	PC
	☐ *Coccyzus merlini santamariae*	LC	CU	Co	Br	YR	-	L
	☐ *Coccyzus merlini decolor*	LC	CU	Co	Br	YR	-	L
1.30. NIGHTHAWKS, NIGHTJARS AND POTOOS								
Order: CAPRIMULGIFORMES Family: Caprimulgidae								
59.	☐ *Chordeiles minor*/**Common Nighthawk**/Querequeté Americano/**CONI**	LC	-	U	-	T	-	P
	☐ *Chordeiles minor minor*	LC	-	U	-	T	-	P
	☐ *Chordeiles minor howelli*	LC	-	VR	-	T	-	P
60.	☐ *Chordeiles gundlachii*/**Antillean Nighthawk**/Querequeté/**ANNI**	LC	-	Co	Br	T-SR	-	PC
	☐ *Chordeiles gundlachii gundlachii*	LC	-	Co	Br	T-SR	-	PC
	☐ *Chordeiles gundlachii vicinus*[5]	LC	-	VR	-	V	-	P
61.	☐ *Antrostomus carolinensis*/**Chuck-will's widow**/Guabairo Americano/**CWWI**	NT	-	FC	-	T-WR	-	PC
62.	☐ *Antrostomus cubanensis*/**Cuban Nightjar**/Guabairo/**no code**[6]	LC	CU	FC	Br	YR	-	PC
	☐ *Antrostomus cubanensis cubanensis*	LC	CU	FC	Br	YR	-	PC
	☐ *Antrostomus cubanensis insulaepinorum*	LC	CU	FC	Br	YR	-	L
63.	☐ *Antrostomus vociferus*/**Eastern Whip-poor-will**/Guabairo Chico/**EWPW**	NT	-	R	-	V	-	P
Order: NYCTIBIIFORMES Family: Nictibiidae								
64.	☐ *Nyctibius jamaicensis ssp. (cf. jamaicensis)*/**Northern Potoo (Caribbean)**/Potú/**NORP**[7]	LC	?	VR	?	YR?	-	P
1.31. SWIFTS AND HUMMINGBIRDS								
Order: APODIFORMES Family: Apodidae								
65.	☐ *Cypseloides niger niger*/**Black Swift (niger)**/Vencejo Negro/**BLSW**[8]	VU	WI	U	Br	T?-YR	-	L
66.	☐ *Streptoprocne zonaris pallidifrons*/**White-collared Swift**/Vencejo de Collar/**WCSW**	LC	WI	U	Br	YR	-	L
67.	☐ *Chaetura pelagica*/**Chimney Swift**/Vencejo de Chimenea/**CHSW**	VU	-	R	-	T	-	P
68.	☐ *Tachornis phoenicobia*/**Antillean Palm-Swift**/Vencejito de Palma/**ANPS**	LC	GA	Co	Br	YR	-	PC
	☐ *Tachornis phoenicobia iradii*	LC	CU	Co	Br	YR	-	PC
Order: APODIFORMES Family: Trochilidae								
69.	☐ *Archilochus colubris*/**Ruby-throated Hummingbird**/Colibrí de Garganta Rubí/**RTHU**	LC	-	U	-	T	-	P

	English Name/Cuban Common Name (CCN)/*Latin Name*/Alpha Code	Threat status	End. Reg.	Abun. status	Breed status	Resid. status	Ext.	Dist.
70.	☐ *Mellisuga helenae*/**Bee Hummingbird**/Zunzuncito/**BEEH**	NT/*VU*	CU	U	Br	YR	-	L
71.	☐ **Nesophlox* sp. (prob. *evelynae*)/**Bahama Woodstar**/Colibrí de Bahamas/**BAWO**	LC	LY	VR	-	V	-	P
72.	☐ *Riccordia ricordii*/**Cuban Emerald**/Zunzún/**CUEM**	LC	CU-LY	Co	Br	YR	-	PC
	1.32. MARSH BIRDS							
	Order: GRUIFORMES Family: Rallidae							
73.	☐ *Cyanolimnas cerverai*/**Zapata Rail**/Gallinuela de Santo Tomás/**ZARA**[9]	CR	CU	XR	Br	YR	-	L
74.	☐ *Pardirallus maculatus* (cf. *insolitus*)/**Spotted Rail**/Gallinuela Escribano/**SPRA**	LC	-	FC	Br	YR	-	QC
75.	☐ *Rallus elegans*/**King Rail**/Gallinuela de Agua Dulce/**KIRA**	NT	-	FC	Br	PM	-	QC
	☐ *Rallus elegans elegans* (**Northern**)	NT	-	R	-	V	-	P
	☐ *Rallus elegans ramsdeni* (**Cuban**)	NT	CU	FC	Br	YR	-	QC
76.	☐ *Rallus crepitans*/**Clapper Rail**/Gallinuela de Manglar/**CLRA**	LC	-	Co	Br	PM	-	PC
	☐ *Rallus crepitans crepitans* (**Atlantic Coast**)	LC	-	VR?	-	V-WR?	-	P
	☐ *Rallus crepitans leucophaeus* (**Caribbean**)	LC	CU	Co	Br	YR	-	L
	☐ *Rallus crepitans caribaeus* (**Caribbean**)	LC	WI	Co	Br	YR	-	PC
77.	☐ *Rallus limicola limicola*/**Virginia Rail (Virginia)**/Gallinuela de Virginia/**VIRA**	LC	-	R	-	V	-	P
78.	☐ *Porzana carolina*/**Sora**/Gallinuela Oscura/**SORA**	LC	-	FC	-	T-WR	-	QC
79.	☐ *Gallinula galeata cerceris*/**Common Gallinule (American)**/Gallareta de Pico Rojo/**COGA**	LC	WI	Co	Br	PM	-	PC
80.	☐ *Fulica americana*/**American Coot**/Gallareta de Pico Blanco/**AMCO**	LC	-	Co	Br	PM	-	PC
81.	☐ *Porphyrio martinicus*/**Purple Gallinule**/Gallareta Azul/**PUGA**	LC	-	Co	Br	PM	-	PC
82.	☐ *Hapalocrex flaviventer gossii*/**Yellow-breasted Crake**/Gallinuelita/**YBCR**	LC	GA	U	Br?	YR?	-	L
83.	☐ *Laterallus jamaicensis jamaicensis*/**Black Rail (Northern)**/Gallinuelita Prieta/**BLRA**	EN	-	R	-?	T-PM[W]	-	QC
	Order: GRUIFORMES Family: Aramidae							
84.	☐ *Aramus guarauna pictus*/**Limpkin (Speckled)**/Guareao/**LIMP**	LC	-	Co	Br	YR	-	PC
	Order: GRUIFORMES Family: Gruidae							
85.	☐ *Antigone canadensis nesiotes*/**Sandhill Crane (nesiotes)**/Grulla/**SACR**	LC/*VU*	CU	U	Br	YR	-	L
	Order: CHARADRIIFORMES Family: Recurvirostridae							
86.	☐ *Himantopus mexicanus mexicanus*/**Black-necked Stilt (Black-necked)**/Cachiporra/**BNST**	LC	-	Co	Br	PM	-	PC

	English Name/Cuban Common Name (CCN)/*Latin Name*/Alpha Code	Threat status	End. Reg.	Abun. status	Breed status	Resid. status	Ext.	Dist.
87.	*Recurvirostra americana*/**American Avocet**/Avoceta Americana/**AMAV**	LC	-	U-FC	Br[10]	T-WR[PM]	-	L
	Order: CHARADRIIFORMES Family: Haematopodidae							
88.	*Haematopus palliatus palliatus*/**American Oystercatcher**/Ostrero/**AMOY**	LC	-	U	Br	T-PM[W]	-	QC
	Order: CHARADRIIFORMES Family: Charadriidae							
89.	*Pluvialis squatarola*/**Black-bellied Plover**/Pluvial Cabezón/**BBPL**	LC	-	Co-U	?	T-WR[PM]	-	QC
90.	*Pluvialis dominica*/**American Golden-Plover**/Pluvial Dorado/**AMGP**	LC	-	R	-	T	-	P
91.	*Charadrius vociferus*/**Killdeer**/Títere Sabanero/**KILL**	LC	-	Co	Br	PM	-	PC
	Charadrius vociferus vociferus	LC	-	FC	-	T-WR	-	PC
	Charadrius vociferus ternominatus	LC	GA	Co	Br	YR	-	PC
92.	*Charadrius semipalmatus*/**Semipalmated Plover**/Frailecillo Semipalmeado/**SEPL**	LC	-	Co	-	T-WR	-	QC
93.	*Charadrius melodus*/**Piping Plover**/Frailecillo Silbador/**PIPL**	NT/VU	-	U	-	T-WR	-	QC
94.	*Charadrius wilsonia wilsonia*/**Wilson's Plover**/Títere Playero/**WIPL**	LC	-	Co	Br	T-PM[S]	-	PC
95.	*Charadrius nivosus nivosus*/**Snowy Plover (nivosus)**/Frailecillo Blanco/**SNPL**	NT/VU	-	R	Br	T-PM[W]	-	L
	Order: CHARADRIIFORMES Family: Jacanidae							
96.	*Jacana spinosa violacea*/**Northern Jacana**/Gallito de Río/**NOJA**	LC	GA	Co	Br	YR	-	PC
	Order: CHARADRIIFORMES Family: Scolopacidae							
97.	*Bartramia longicauda*/**Upland Sandpiper**/Ganga/**UPSA**	LC	-	R	-	T	-	P
98.	*Numenius phaeopus*/**Whimbrel**/Zarapico Pico de Cimitarra Chico/**WHIM**	LC	-	U	-	V-T-WR	-	P
	Numenius phaeopus phaeopus (**European**)	LC	-	VR	-	V	-	P
	Numenius phaeopus hudsonicus (**Hudsonian**)	LC	-	U	-	T-WR	-	P
99.	*Numenius americanus americanus*/**Long-billed Curlew**/Zarapico Pico de Cimitarra Grande/**LBCU**	LC	-	R	-	V	-	P
100.	*Limosa haemastica*/**Hudsonian Godwit**/Avoceta Pechirroja/**HUGO**	LC	-	R	-	V	-	P
101.	*Limosa fedoa* (prob. *fedoa*)/**Marbled Godwit**/Avoceta Parda/**MAGO**	LC	-	R	-	V	-	P
102.	*Arenaria interpres morinella*/**Ruddy Turnstone**/Revuelvepiedras/**RUTU**	LC	-	Co	?	T-PM[W]	-	PC
103.	*Calidris canutus* ssp./**Red Knot**/Zarapico Raro/**REKN**	NT	-	U	-	T-WR	-	P
104.	*Calidris pugnax*/**Ruff**/Combatiente (SEO)/**RUFF**	LC	-	VR	-	V	-	P
105.	*Calidris himantopus*/**Stilt Sandpiper**/Zarapico Patilargo/**STSA**	LC	-	FC	-	T-WR	-	QC

	English Name/Cuban Common Name (CCN)/*Latin Name*/Alpha Code	Threat status	End. Reg.	Abun. status	Breed status	Resid. status	Ext.	Dist.
106.	☐ *Calidris alba*/**Sanderling**/Zarapico Blanco/**SAND**	LC	-	Co	-	T-WR	-	PC
107.	☐ *Calidris alpina* (prob. *hudsonia*)/**Dunlin**/Zarapico Gris/**DUNL**	LC	-	U-R	-	T-WR	-	P
108.	☐ *Calidris minutilla*/**Least Sandpiper**/Zarapiquito/**LESA**	LC	-	Co	-	T-WR	-	PC
109.	☐ *Calidris fuscicollis*/**White-rumped Sandpiper**/Zarapico de Rabadilla Blanca/**WRSA**	LC	-	FC	-	T[11]	-	P
110.	☐ *Calidris subruficollis*/**Buff-breasted Sandpiper**/Zarapico Piquicorto/**BBSA**	NT	-	VR	-	V	-	P
111.	☐ *Calidris melanotos*/**Pectoral Sandpiper**/Zarapico Moteado/**PESA**	LC	-	U-R	-	T-WR	-	P
112.	☐ *Calidris pusilla*/**Semipalmated Sandpiper**/Zarapico Semipalmeado/**SESA**	NT	-	Co	-	T-WR	-	PC
113.	☐ *Calidris mauri*/**Western Sandpiper**/Zarapico Chico/**WESA**	LC	-	FC-U	-	T-WR?	-	L
114.	☐ *Limnodromus griseus*/**Short-billed Dowitcher**/Zarapico Becasina/**SBDO**	LC	-	Co	-	T-WR	-	QC
	☐ *Limnodromus griseus griseus* (**griseus**)	LC	-	Co	-	T-WR	-	QC
	☐ *Limnodromus griseus hendersoni* (**hendersoni**)	LC	-	U?	-	T-WR?	-	P?
115.	☐ *Limnodromus scolopaceus*/**Long-billed Dowitcher**/Zarapico Becasina de Pico Largo/**LBDO**	LC	-	FC	-	T-WR	-	L
116.	☐ *Gallinago delicata*/**Wilson's Snipe**/Becasina/**WISN**	LC	-	FC	-	T-WR	-	PC
117.	☐ *Actitis macularius*/**Spotted Sandpiper**/Zarapico Manchado/**SPSA**	LC	-	Co	-	T-WR	-	PC
118.	☐ *Tringa solitaria solitaria*/**Solitary Sandpiper (solitaria)**/Zarapico Solitario/**SOSA**	LC	-	FC	-	T-WR	-	QC
119.	☐ *Tringa flavipes*/**Lesser Yellowlegs**/Zarapico Patiamarillo Chico/**LEYE**	LC	-	Co	?	T-WR[PM]	-	PC
120.	☐ *Tringa semipalmata*/**Willet**/Zarapico Real/**WILL**	LC	-	Co	Br	PM	-	PC
	☐ *Tringa semipalmata semipalmata* (**Eastern**)	LC	-	Co	?	PM[W]	-	PC
	☐ *Tringa semipalmata inornata* (**Western**)	LC	-	Co?	Br	WR?	-	QC
121.	☐ *Tringa melanoleuca*/**Greater Yellowlegs**/Zarapico Patiamarillo Grande/**GRYE**	LC	-	Co	?	T-PM[W]	-	PC
122.	☐ *Phalaropus tricolor*/**Wilson's Phalarope**/Zarapico de Wilson/**WIPH**	LC	-	R	-	V	-	P
123.	☐ *Phalaropus lobatus*/**Red-necked Phalarope**/Zarapico Nadador/**RNPH**[12]	LC	-	VR	-	V	-	P
124.	☐ *Phalaropus fulicarius*/**Red Phalarope**/Zarapico Rojo/**REPH**	LC	-	VR	-	V	-	P

1.33. GULLLIKE BIRDS

Order: CHARADRIIFORMES   Family: Stercorariidae

125.	☐ *Stercorarius maccormicki*/**South Polar Skua**/Skua del Polo Sur/**SPSK**	LC	-	VR	-	V	-	OW-P

	English Name/Cuban Common Name (CCN)/*Latin Name*/Alpha Code	Threat status	End. Reg.	Abun. status	Breed status	Resid. status	Ext.	Dist.
126.	*Stercorarius pomarinus*/**Pomarine Jaeger**/Estercorario Pomarino/**POJA**[13]	LC	-	R	-	V-WR?	-	OW-P
127.	*Stercorarius parasiticus*/**Parasitic Jaeger**/Estercorario Parasítico/**PAJA**	LC	-	R	-	V	-	OW-P
128.	*Stercorarius longicaudus* (prob. *pallescens*)/**Long-tailed Jaeger**/Estercorario Rabero/**LTJA**	LC	-	VR	-	V	-	OW-P
	Order: CHARADRIIFORMES Family: Alcidae							
129.	*Alle alle alle*/**Dovekie**/Pingüinito/**DOVE**	LC	-	R	-	V	-	OW-P
	Order: CHARADRIIFORMES Family: Laridae							
130.	*Rissa tridactyla* (prob. *tridactyla*)/**Black-legged Kittiwake (tridactyla)**/Gallego Patinegro/**BLKI**[14]	VU	-	R	-	V	-	P
131.	*Xema sabini sabini*/**Sabine's Gull**/Gallego de Cola Ahorquillada/**SAGU**[15]	LC	-	VR	-	V	-	P
132.	*Chroicocephalus philadelphia*/**Bonaparte's Gull**/Galleguito Chico/**BOGU**	LC	-	R	-	T-WR	-	P
133.	*Chroicocephalus ridibundus*/**Black-headed Gull**/Galleguito Raro/**BHGU**	LC	-	VR	-	V	-	P
134.	*Leucophaeus atricilla atricilla*/**Laughing Gull**/Galleguito/**LAGU**	LC	-	Co	Br	T-PM[W]	-	PC
135.	*Leucophaeus pipixcan*/**Franklin's Gull**/Galleguito de Franklin/**FRGU**	LC	-	R	-	V	-	P
136.	*Larus delawarensis*/**Ring-billed Gull**/Gallego Real/**RBGU**[16]	LC	-	FC	-	T-WR	-	P
137.	*Larus argentatus smithsonianus*/**Herring Gull (American)**/Gallego/**HERG**	LC	-	FC	-	T-WR	-	QC
138.	*Larus fuscus graellsii*/**Lesser Black-backed Gull**/Gallego Pequeño de Espalda Negra/**LBBG**	LC	-	R	-	WR	-	P
139.	*Larus marinus*/**Great Black-backed Gull**/Gallegón/**GBBG**	LC	-	VR	-	WR	-	P
140.	*Anous stolidus stolidus*/**Brown Noddy**/Gaviota Boba/**BRNO**	LC	-	FC	Br	T-SR	-	OW-L
141.	*Onychoprion fuscatus fuscatus*/**Sooty Tern**/Gaviota Monja Prieta/**SOTE**	LC	-	FC	Br	T-PM[S]	-	L
142.	*Onychoprion anaethetus melanopterus* (*recognitus*)/**Bridled Tern**/Gaviota Monja/**BRTE**	LC	-	Co	Br	SR[PM]	-	L
143.	*Sternula antillarum antillarum*/**Least Tern**/Gaviotica/**LETE**	LC	-	Co	Br	T-PM[S]	-	QC
144.	*Phaetusa simplex* (prob. *simplex*)/**Large-billed Tern**/Gaviota de Pico Largo/**LBTE**	LC	-	VR	-	V	-	P
145.	*Gelochelidon nilotica aranea*/**Gull-billed Tern (Gull-billed)**/Gaviota de Pico Corto/**GBTE**	LC	-	FC	Br	T-PM[W]	-	PC
146.	*Hydroprogne caspia*/**Caspian Tern**/Gaviota Real Grande/**CATE**	LC	-	FC	?	T-PM[W]	-	QC

	English Name/Cuban Common Name (CCN)/*Latin Name*/Alpha Code	Threat status	End. Reg.	Abun. status	Breed status	Resid. status	Ext.	Dist.
147.	*Chlidonias niger surinamensis*/**Black Tern (American)**/Gaviotica Prieta/**BLTE**	LC	-	R	-	T	-	QC
148.	*Sterna dougallii dougallii*/**Roseate Tern**/Gaviota Rosada/**ROST**	LC/*VU*	-	R	Br	T-SR[PM]	-	P
149.	*Sterna hirundo hirundo*/**Common Tern (hirundo/tibetana)**/Gaviota Común/**COTE**	LC	-	U	?	T-WR	-	PC
150.	*Sterna paradisaea*/**Arctic Tern**/Gaviota Ártica/**ARTE**[17]	LC	-	VR	-	V	-	P
151.	*Sterna forsteri*/**Forster's Tern**/Gaviota de Forster/**FOTE**	LC	-	U	-	WR	-	P
152.	*Thalasseus maximus maximus*/**Royal Tern**/Gaviota Real/**ROYT**	LC	-	Co	Br	T-PM[W]	-	PC
153.	*Thalasseus sandvicensis*/**Sandwich Tern**/Gaviota de Pico Amarillo/**SATE**	LC	-	FC	Br	T-PM[S]	-	QC
	Thalasseus sandvicensis acuflavidus (Cabot's)	LC	-	FC	Br	PM[S]	-	QC
	Thalasseus sandvicensis eurygnatus (Cayenne)	LC	-	VR	Br	T-SR	-	L
154.	*Rynchops niger niger*/**Black Skimmer (niger)**/Gaviota Pico de Tijera/**BLSK**	LC	-	FC	-	T-WR	-	QC
	Order: PHAETHONTIFORMES Family: Phaethontidae							
155.	*Phaethon lepturus catesbyi*/**White-tailed Tropicbird (Atlantic)**/Contramaestre/**WTTR**	LC	-	R	Br	PM[S]	-	OW-L
156.	*Phaethon aethereus mesonauta*/**Red-billed Tropicbird**/Rabijunco de Pico Rojo/**RBTR**	LC	-	R	-	V	-	OW-P
	Order: GAVIIFORMES Family: Gaviidae							
157.	*Gavia immer*/**Common Loon**/Somormujo/**COLO**	LC	-	R	-	V	-	P
	Order: PROCELLARIIFORMES Family: Oceanitidae							
158.	*Oceanites oceanicus oceanicus*/**Wilson's Storm-Petrel (Wilson's)**/Pamperito de Wilson/**WISP**	LC	-	R	-	V	-	OW-P
	Order: PROCELLARIIFORMES Family: Hydrobatidae							
159.	*Hydrobates leucorhous leucorhous*/**Leach's Storm-Petrel (Leach´s)**/Pamperito de las Tempestades/**LESP**	VU	-	VR	-	V	-	OW-P
160.	*Hydrobates castro*/**Band-rumped Storm-Petrel**/Pamperito de Castro/**BSTP**	LC	-	VR	-	V	-	OW-P
	Order: PROCELLARIIFORMES Family: Procellariidae							
161.	*Pterodroma hasitata*/**Black-capped Petrel**/Pájaro de la Bruja/**BCPE**	EN	-	R	?	?	-	OW-L
162.	*Calonectris diomedea borealis*/**Cory's Shearwater (borealis)**/Pampero de Cory/**CORS**	LC	-	R	-	V	-	OW-P
163.	*Ardenna grisea*/**Sooty Shearwater**/Pampero Oscuro/**SOSH**	NT	-	R	-	V	-	OW-P
164.	*Ardenna gravis*/**Great Shearwater**/Pampero Grande/**GRSH**	LC	-	VR	-	V	-	OW-P
165.	*Puffinus lherminieri lherminieri*/**Audubon's Shearwater**/Pampero de Audubon/**AUSH**	LC	-	R	Br	YR-PM?	-	OW-P
	Order: CICONIIFORMES Family: Ciconiidae							
166.	*Mycteria americana*/**Wood Stork**/Cayama/**WOST**	LC	-	R	Br	YR	-	L

	English Name/Cuban Common Name (CCN)/*Latin Name*/Alpha Code	Threat status	End. Reg.	Abun. status	Breed status	Resid. status	Ext.	Dist.
	Order: SULIFORMES Family: Fregatidae							
167.	*Fregata magnificens*/**Magnificent Frigatebird**/Rabihorcado/**MAFR**	LC	-	Co	Br	YR	-	PC
	Order: SULIFORMES Family: Sulidae							
168.	*Sula dactylatra dactylatra*/**Masked Booby**/Pájaro Bobo de Cara Azul/**MABO**	LC	-	U	-	YR	-	OW
169.	*Sula leucogaster leucogaster*/**Brown Booby (Atlantic)**/Pájaro Bobo Prieto/**BRBO**	LC	-	FC	Br	YR	-	OW
170.	*Sula sula sula*/**Red-footed Booby (Atlantic)**/Pájaro Bobo Blanco/**RFBO**	LC	-	R	-	YR	-	OW
171.	**Morus bassanus*/**Northern Gannet**/Albatros/**NOGA**	LC	-	VR	-	V	-	P
	Order: SULIFORMES Family: Anhingidae							
172.	*Anhinga anhinga leucogaster*/**Anhinga**/Marbella/**ANHI**	LC	-	Co	Br	YR	-	PC
	Order: SULIFORMES Family: Phalacrocoracidae							
173.	*Nannopterum auritum*/**Double-crested Cormorant**/Corúa de Mar/**DCCO**	LC	-	Co	Br	PM	-	PC
	Nannopterum auritum auritum	LC	-	R?	-	V	-	P
	Nannopterum auritum floridanus	LC	-	Co	Br	YR	-	PC
	Nannopterum auritum heuretus	LC	-	R?	-	V?	-	L?
174.	*Nannopterum brasilianum mexicanus*/**Neotropic Cormorant**/Corúa de Agua Dulce/**NECO**	LC	-	Co	Br	YR	-	PC
	Order: PELECANIFORMES Family: Pelecanidae							
175.	*Pelecanus erythrorhynchos*/**American White Pelican**/Pelícano Blanco/**AWPE**	LC	-	FC	-	WR^{PM}	-	QC
176.	*Pelecanus occidentalis*/**Brown Pelican**/Pelícano/**BRPE**	LC	-	Co	Br	YR	-	PC
	Pelecanus occidentalis occidentalis (Southern)	LC	-	Co	Br	YR	-	QC
	Pelecanus occidentalis carolinensis (Atlantic)	LC	-	FC	?	PM?	-	PC
	1.34. HERONLIKE BIRDS							
	Order: PELECANIFORMES Family: Ardeidae							
177.	*Botaurus lentiginosus*/**American Bittern**/Guanabá Rojo/**AMBI**	LC	-	U	-?	T-WR	-	QC
178.	*Ixobrychus exilis exilis*/**Least Bittern**/Garcita/**LEBI**	LC	-	FC	Br	T-PM^W	-	PC
179.	*Ardea herodias*/**Great Blue Heron**/Garcilote Azul/**GBHE**	LC	-	Co	Br	PM	-	PC
	Ardea herodias herodias (Great Blue)	LC	-	Co	-	T-WR	-	QC
	Ardea herodias wardi (Great Blue)	LC	-	Co	Br	YR/PM?	-	L
	Ardea herodias occidentalis (Great White)	EN	-	Co	Br	PM	-	L
180.	*Ardea alba egretta*/**Great Egret (American)**/Garzón/**GREG**	LC	-	Co	Br	T-PM	-	PC
181.	*Egretta thula thula*/**Snowy Egret**/Garza Real/**SNEG**	LC	-	Co	Br	T-PM	-	PC
182.	*Egretta caerulea*/**Little Blue Heron**/Garza Azul/**LBHE**	LC	-	Co	Br	T-PM	-	PC
183.	*Egretta tricolor ruficollis*/**Tricolored Heron**/Garza de Vientre Blanco/**TRHE**	LC	-	Co	Br	T-PM	-	PC

	English Name/Cuban Common Name (CCN)/*Latin Name*/Alpha Code	Threat status	End. Reg.	Abun. status	Breed status	Resid. status	Ext.	Dist.
184.	*Egretta rufescens rufescens*/**Reddish Egret**/Garza Rojiza/**REEG**	NT	-	FC	Br	T-PM	-	QC
185.	*Bubulcus ibis ibis*/**Cattle Egret (Western)**/Garcita Bueyera/**CAEG**	LC	-	Co	Br	PM	-	PC
186.	*Butorides virescens virescens*/**Green Heron** (*virescens/bahamensis*)/Aguaitacaimán/**GRHE**[18]	LC	-	Co	Br	PM	-	PC
187.	*Nycticorax nycticorax hoactli*/**Black-crowned Night-Heron (American)**/Guanabá de la Florida/**BCNH**	LC	-	Co	Br	T-PM	-	PC
188.	*Nyctanassa violacea*/**Yellow-crowned Night-Heron**/Guanabá Real/**YCNH**	LC	-	Co	Br	PM[W]	-	PC
	Nyctanassa violacea violacea (Yellow-crowned Group)	LC	-	U	-	T-WR	-	QC
	Nyctanassa violacea bancrofti (Yellow-crowned Group)	LC	-	Co	Br	PM	-	PC
	Order: PELECANIFORMES Family: Threskiornithidae							
189.	*Eudocimus albus*/**White Ibis**/Coco Blanco/**WHIB**	LC	-	Co	Br	T-PM	-	PC
190.	*Eudocimus ruber*/**Scarlet Ibis**/Coco Rojo/**SCIB**	LC	-	VR	-	V	-	P
191.	*Plegadis falcinellus*/**Glossy Ibis**/Coco Prieto/**GLIB**	LC	-	Co	Br	T-PM	-	PC
192.	*Plegadis chihi*/**White-faced Ibis**/Coco Cariblanco/**WFIB**[19]	LC	-	VR	-	V	-	P
193.	*Platalea ajaja*/**Roseate Spoonbill**/Sevilla/**ROSP**	LC	-	Co	Br	PM	-	PC
	1.35. HAWKLIKE BIRDS							
	Order: CATHARTIFORMES Family: Cathartidae							
194.	*Coragyps atratus atratus*/**Black Vulture**/Zopilote/**BLVU**[20]	LC	-	R	?	PM	-	L
195.	*Cathartes aura*/**Turkey Vulture (Northern)**/Aura Tiñosa/**TUVU**	LC	-	Co	Br	PM	-	PC
	Cathartes aura aura	LC	-	Co	Br	PM	-	PC
	Cathartes aura septentrionalis	LC	-	U?	-?	T?-WR?	-	P
	Order: ACCIPITRIFORMES Family: Pandionidae							
196.	*Pandion haliaetus*/**Osprey**/Guincho/**OSPR**	LC	-	Co	Br	PM[W]	-	PC
	(*carolinensis*)/*Pandion haliaetus carolinensis*	LC	-	Co	-	T-WR	-	PC
	(*ridgwayi*)/*Pandion haliaetus ridgwayi*	LC	-	U	Br	YR	-	L
	Order: ACCIPITRIFORMES Family: Accipitridae							
197.	*Chondrohierax wilsonii*/**Cuban Kite**/Gavilán Caguarero/**no code**[21]	CR	CU	XR	Br	YR	-	L
198.	*Elanoides forficatus forficatus*/**Swallow-tailed Kite**/Gavilán Cola de Tijera/**STKI**	LC	-	FC	-	T	-	L
199.	*Circus hudsonicus*/**Northern Harrier**/Gavilán Sabanero/**NOHA**	LC	-	FC	-	T-WR	-	PC
200.	*Accipiter striatus*/**Sharp-shinned Hawk**/Gavilancito/**SSHA**	LC	-	U	Br	YR	-	PC
	Accipiter striatus velox (Northern)	LC	-	U	-	T-WR?	-	PC
	Accipiter striatus fringilloides (Caribbean)[22]	LC	CU	U	Br	YR	-	QC

	English Name/Cuban Common Name (CCN)/*Latin Name*/Alpha Code	Threat status	End. Reg.	Abun. status	Breed status	Resid. status	Ext.	Dist.
201.	☐ ****Accipiter cooperi*/**Cooper´s Hawk**/Gavilán de Cooper/**COHA**	LC	-	VR	-	T	-	P
202.	☐ *Accipiter gundlachi*/**Gundlach's Hawk**/Gavilán Colilargo/**GUHA**[23]	EN	CU	U	Br	YR	-	PC
	☐ *Accipiter gundlachi gundlachi*	EN	CU	U	Br	YR	-	QC
	☐ *Accipiter gundlachi wileyi*[24]	EN	CU	U	Br	YR	-	Rg
203.	☐ *Haliaeetus leucocephalus leucocephalus*/**Bald Eagle**/Águila Calva/**BAEA**	LC	-	R	-	V	-	P
204.	☐ *Ictinia mississippiensis*/**Mississippi Kite**/Gavilán del Mississippi/**MIKI**	LC	-	U-FC?	-	T	-	P
205.	☐ *Rostrhamus sociabilis plumbeus*/**Snail Kite**/Gavilán Caracolero/**SNKI**	LC	-	FC	Br	YR	-	PC
206.	☐ *Buteogallus gundlachii*/**Cuban Black Hawk**/Gavilán Batista/**CUBH**	NT/*EN*	CU	FC	Br	YR	-	QC
207.	☐ *Buteo platypterus*/**Broad-winged Hawk**/Gavilán Bobo/**BWHA**	LC	-	Co	Br	PM[W]	-	PC
	☐ *Buteo platypterus platypterus* (**Northern**)	LC	-	U?	-	T-WR	-	P
	☐ *Buteo platypterus cubanensis* (**Caribbean**)	LC	CU	Co	Br	YR	-	PC
208.	☐ ****Buteo brachyurus* (prob. *fuliginosus*)/**Short-tailed Hawk**/Gavilán de Cola Corta/**STHA**	LC	-	R	-	T	-	P
209.	☐ *Buteo swainsoni*/**Swainson's Hawk**/Gavilán de Swainson/**SWHA**[25]	LC	-	R	-	T	-	P
210.	☐ *Buteo jamaicensis solitudinis*/**Red-tailed Hawk**/Gavilán de Monte/**RTHA**	LC	CU-LY	Co	Br	PM? -YR	-	PC
1.36. OWLS								
Order: STRIGIFORMES Family: Tytonidae								
211.	☐ *Tyto alba*/**Barn Owl**/Lechuza/**BANO**	LC	-	Co	Br	YR	-	PC
	☐ *Tyto alba pratincola* (**American**)	LC	-	VR	Br	V-WR?	-	P
	☐ *Tyto alba furcata* (**White-winged**)	LC	GA	Co	Br	YR	-	PC
Order: STRIGIFORMES Family: Strigidae								
212.	☐ *Margarobyas lawrencii lawrencii*/**Bare-legged Owl**/Sijú Cotunto/**BLOW**	LC	CU	FC	Br	YR	-	PC
213.	☐ *Glaucidium siju*/**Cuban Pygmy-Owl**/Sijú Platanero/**CUPO**	LC	CU	Co	Br	YR	-	PC
	☐ *Glaucidium siju siju*	LC	CU	Co	Br	YR	-	PC
	☐ *Glaucidium siju vittatum*	LC	CU	Co	Br	YR	-	L
	☐ *Glaucidium siju turquinense*	LC	CU	Co	Br	YR	-	L
214.	☐ *Athene cunicularia*/**Burrowing Owl**/Sijú de Sabana/**BUOW**	LC	-	U	Br	YR[W]	-	L
	☐ *Athene cunicularia floridana* (**Florida**)	LC	-	R	-	WR	-	P
	☐ *Athene cunicularia guantanamensis* (**guadeloupensis Group**)[26]	LC	CU	U	Br	YR	-	L

	English Name/Cuban Common Name (CCN)/*Latin Name*/Alpha Code	Threat status	End. Reg.	Abun. status	Breed status	Resid. status	Ext.	Dist.
215.	☐ *Asio otus wilsonianus*/**Long-eared Owl (American)**/Buho Chico (SEO)/**LEOW**	LC	-	VR	-	V	-	P
216.	☐ *Asio stygius siguapa*/**Stygian Owl**/Siguapa/**STOW**	LC	CU	U	Br	YR	-	PC
217.	☐ *Asio flammeus domingensis*/**Short-eared Owl (Antillean)**/Cárabo/**SEOW**	LC	GA	FC	Br	YR	-	PC

1.37. TROGONS, TODIES AND ALLIES
Order: TROGONIFORMES   Family: Trogonidae

218.	☐ *Priotelus temnurus*/**Cuban Trogon**/Tocororo/**CUTR**	LC	CU	Co	Br	YR	-	PC
	Priotelus temnurus temnurus	LC	CU	Co	Br	YR	-	PC
	Priotelus temnurus vescus	LC	CU	Co	Br	YR	-	L

Order: CORACIIFORMES   Family: Todidae

219.	☐ *Todus multicolor*/**Cuban Tody**/Cartacuba/**CUTO**	LC	CU	Co	Br	YR	-	PC

Order: CORACIIFORMES   Family: Alcedinidae

220.	☐ *Megaceryle alcyon*/**Belted Kingfisher**/Martín Pescador/**BEKI**	LC	-	Co	-	T-WR	-	PC

1.38. WOODPECKERS
Order: PICIFORMES   Family: Picidae

221.	☐ *Melanerpes superciliaris*/**West Indian Woodpecker**/Carpintero Jabado/**WIWO**	LC	GA-LY	Co	Br	YR	-	PC
	Melanerpes superciliaris superciliaris	LC	CU	Co	Br	YR	-	PC
	Melanerpes superciliaris murceus	LC	CU	Co	Br	YR	-	L
222.	☐ *Sphyrapicus varius*/**Yellow-bellied Sapsucker**/Carpintero de Paso/**YBSA**	LC	-	FC	-	T-WR	-	PC
223.	☐ *Xiphidiopicus percussus*/**Cuban Green Woodpecker**/Carpintero Verde/**CGWO**	LC	CU	Co	Br	YR	-	PC
	Xiphidiopicus percussus percussus	LC	CU	Co	Br	YR	-	PC
	Xiphidiopicus percussus insulaepinorum	LC	CU	Co	Br	YR	-	L
224.	☐ *Colaptes auratus chrysocaulosus*/**Northern Flicker (Cuban)**/Carpintero Escapulario/**NOFL**	LC	CU	FC	Br	YR	-	PC
225.	☐ *Colaptes fernandinae*/**Fernandina's Flicker**/Carpintero Churroso/**FEFL**	EN/*VU*	CU	U	Br	YR	-	L
226.	☐ *Dryocopus pileatus*/**Pileated Woodpeaker**/Carpintero Norteamericano/**PIWO**[27]	LC	-	VR	-	V	-	P
227.	☐ *Campephilus principalis bairdii*/**Ivory-billed Woodpecker (Cuban)**/Carpintero Real/**IBWO**	CR (Ex?)	CU	XR	Br	YR	-	L

1.39. FALCONS AND ALLIES
Order: FALCONIFORMES   Family: Falconidae

228.	☐ *Caracara plancus cheriway*/**Crested Caracara**/Caraira/**CRCA**[28]	LC	-	FC	Br	YR	-	QC
229.	☐ *Falco sparverius*/**American Kestrel**/Cernícalo/**AMKE**	LC	-	Co	Br	YR^w	-	PC
	Falco sparverius sparverius (Northern)	LC	-	FC	-	T-WR	-	PC
	Falco sparverius sparverioides (Cuban)	LC	GA	Co	Br	YR	-	PC

English Name/Cuban Common Name (CCN)/*Latin Name*/Alpha Code	Threat status	End. Reg.	Abun. status	Breed status	Resid. status	Ext.	Dist.
230. ☐ *Falco columbarius columbarius*/**Merlin (Taiga)**/Halcón de Palomas/**MERL**	LC	-	Co	-	T-WR	-	PC
231. ☐ *Falco peregrinus*/**Peregrine Falcon**/Halcón Peregrino/**PEFA**	LC	-	FC	-	T-WR	-	PC
☐ *Falco peregrinus anatum* (North American)	LC	-	FC	Br?	T-WR-PM?	-	PC
☐ *Falco peregrinus tundrius* (tundrius)	LC	-	U	-	T	-	P

1.40. PARROTS AND PARAKEETS
Order: PSITTACIFORMES   Family: Psittacidae

232. ☐ *Ara ararauna*/**Blue-and-yellow Macaw**/Guacamayo Azul y Amarillo/**BAYM**	LC	-	U	Br	YR	**P-C7**	L
233. ☐ *Ara tricolor*/**Cuban Macaw**/Guacamayo Cubano/**CUBM**	Ex	CU	-	-	-	-	-
234. ☐ *Ara macao ssp.*/**Scarlet Macaw**/Guacamayo Rojo/**SCMA**	LC	-	U	Br	YR	**P-C7**	L
235. ☐ *Ara chloropterus*/**Red-and-green Macaw**/Guacamayo Rojo y Azul/**RAGM**	LC	-	U	Br	YR	**P-C7**	L
236. ☐ *Psittacara euops*/**Cuban Parakeet**/Catey/**CPAK**	VU/*EN*	CU	U	Br	YR	-	L
237. ☐ *Amazona leucocephala*/**Cuban Parrot (Cuban)**/Cotorra/**CPAT**	NT	GA	FC	Br	YR	-	QC
☐ *Amazona leucocephala leucocephala*	NT/*VU*	CU	FC	Br	YR	-	QC

1.41. FLYCATCHERS AND ALLIES
Order: PASSERIFORMES   Family: Tyrannidae

238. ☐ *Myiarchus crinitus*/**Great Crested Flycatcher**/Bobito de Cresta/**GCFL**	LC	-	R	-	T	-	P
239. ☐ *Myiarchus sagrae*/**La Sagra's Flycatcher**/Bobito Grande/**LSFL**	LC	GA/LY	Co	Br	YR	-	PC
☐ *Myiarchus sagrae sagrae*	LC	CU	Co	Br	YR	-	PC
240. ☐ *Tyrannus melancholicus satrapa*/**Tropical Kingbird**/Pitirre Tropical/**TRKI**	LC	-	R	-	V	-	P
241. ☐ *Tyrannus vociferans vociferans*/**Cassin's Kingbird**/Pitirre de Cassin/**CAKI**	LC	-	XR	-	V	-	P
242. ☐ *Tyrannus verticalis*/**Western Kingbird**/Pitirre del Oeste/**WEKI**	LC	-	R	-	V	-	P
243. ☐ *Tyrannus tyrannus*/**Eastern Kingbird**/Pitirre Americano/**EAKI**	LC	-	U	-	T	-	PC
244. ☐ *Tyrannus dominicensis dominicensis*/**Gray Kingbird**/Pitirre Abejero/**GRAK**	LC	-	Co	Br	T-SR	-	PC
245. ☐ *Tyrannus caudifasciatus*/**Loggerhead Kingbird (Loggerhead)**/Pitirre Guatíbere/**LOKI**	LC	GA/LY	Co	Br	YR	-	PC
☐ *Tyrannus caudifasciatus caudifasciatus*	LC	CU	Co	Br	YR	-	PC
246. ☐ *Tyrannus cubensis*/**Giant Kingbird**/Pitirre Real/**GIKI**	EN	CU-LY †	U	Br	YR	-	QC
247. ☐ *Tyrannus forficatus*/**Scissor-tailed Flycatcher**/Bobito Cola de Tijera/**STFL**	LC	-	R	-	V	-	P

	English Name/Cuban Common Name (CCN)/*Latin Name*/Alpha Code	Threat status	End. Reg.	Abun. status	Breed status	Resid. status	Ext.	Dist.
248.	*Tyrannus savana* ssp? /**Fork-tailed Flycatcher**/Pitirre de Cola Ahorquillada/**FTFL**[29]	LC	-	VR	-	V	-	P
249.	*Contopus sordidulus* (prob. *saturatus*)/**Western Wood-Pewee**/Bobito de Bosque del Oeste/**WEWP**	LC	-	R	-	T	-	P
250.	*Contopus virens*/**Eastern Wood-Pewee**/Bobito de Bosque del Este/**EAWP**	LC	-	FC	-	T-WR?	-	QC
251.	*Contopus caribaeus*/**Cuban Pewee**/Bobito Chico/**CUPE**	LC	CU-LY	Co	Br	YR	-	PC
	Contopus caribaeus caribaeus	LC	CU	Co	Br	YR	-	PC
	Contopus caribaeus morenoi	LC	CU	Co	Br	YR	-	L
	Contopus caribaeus nerlyi	LC	CU	Co	Br	YR	-	L
252.	*Empidonax flaviventris*/**Yellow-bellied Flycatcher**/Bobito Amarillo/**YBFL**	LC	-	R	-	T	-	P
253.	*Empidonax virescens*/**Acadian Flycatcher**/Bobito Verde/**ACFL**	LC	-	U	-	T	-	P
254.	*Empidonax alnorum*/**Alder Flycatcher**/Bobito de los Alisos/**ALFL**	LC	-	VR	-	T	-	P
255.	*Empidonax traillii*/**Willow Flycatcher**/Bobito de los Sauces[30]/**WIFL**	LC	-	VR	-	T	-	P
256.	*Empidonax minimus*/**Least Flycatcher**/Bobito Chico Americano/**LEFL**	LC	-	VR	-	V	-	P
257.	*Sayornis phoebe*/**Eastern Phoebe**/Bobito Americano/**EAPH**	LC	-	R	-	V-WR?	-	P
258.	*Pyrocephalus rubinus* (prob. *blatteus*)/**Vermilion Flycatcher (Northern?)**/Bobito Bermellón/**VEFL**	LC	-	XR	-	V	-	P
	**1.42. VIREOS AND CROWS**							
	Order: PASSERIFORMES Family: Vireonidae							
259.	*Vireo griseus*/**White-eyed Vireo**/Vireo de Ojo Blanco/**WEVI**	LC	-	FC	-	T-WR	-	PC
	Vireo griseus griseus (White-eyed)	LC	-	R	-	T-WR	-	PC
	Vireo griseus noveboracensis (White-eyed)	LC	-	FC	-	T-WR	-	QC
260.	*Vireo crassirostris*/**Thick-billed Vireo**/Vireo de Bahamas/**TBVI**	**LC**	CU	U	Br	YR	-	L
	Vireo crassirostris cubensis	VU	CU	U	Br	YR	-	L
261.	*Vireo gundlachii*/**Cuban Vireo**/Juan Chiví/**CUVI**	LC	CU	Co	Br	YR	-	PC
262.	*Vireo flavifrons*/**Yellow-throated Vireo**/Verdón de Pecho Amarillo/**YTVI**	LC	-	FC	-	T-WR	-	PC
263.	*Vireo solitarius solitarius*/**Blue-headed Vireo**/Verdón de Cabeza Gris/**BHVI**	LC	-	R	-	T-WR	-	PC
264.	*Vireo philadelphicus*/**Philadelphia Vireo**/Vireo de Filadelfia/**PHVI**	LC	-	R	-	T-WR?	-	P
265.	*Vireo gilvus gilvus*/**Warbling Vireo**/Vireo Cantor/**WAVI**	LC	-	R	-	T	-	P

	English Name/Cuban Common Name (CCN)/*Latin Name*/Alpha Code	Threat status	End. Reg.	Abun. status	Breed status	Resid. status	Ext.	Dist.
266.	*Vireo olivaceus*/**Red-eyed Vireo**/Vireo de Ojo Rojo/**REVI**	LC	-	FC	-	T-WR	-	PC
267.	*Vireo altiloquus barbatulus*/**Black-whiskered Vireo**/Bien-te-veo/**BWVI**	LC	-	Co	Br	T-SR	-	PC
	Order: PASSERIFORMES Family: Laniidae							
268.	*Lanius* sp. prob. *ludovicianus*/**Shrike sp. (probably Loggerhead Shrike)**/Alcaudón (prob. Americano)[31]	-	-	VR	-	V	-	P
	Order: PASSERIFORMES Family: Corvidae							
269.	*Corvus palmarum*/**Palm Crow (Cuban)**/Cao Pinalero/**PACR**	LC	GA	U	Br	YR	-	L
	Corvus palmarum minutus	EN	CU	U	Br	YR	-	L
270.	*Corvus nasicus*/**Cuban Crow**/Cao Montero/**CUCR**	LC	CU-LY	FC	Br	YR	-	L
	1.43. SWALLOWS							
	Order: PASSERIFORMES Family: Hirundinidae							
271.	*Riparia riparia riparia*/**Bank Swallow**/Golondrina de Collar/**BANS**	LC	-	U	-	T-WR	-	PC
272.	*Tachycineta bicolor*/**Tree Swallow**/Golondrina de Árboles/**TRES**	LC	-	Co	-	T-WR	-	PC
273.	*Tachycineta cyaneoviridis*/**Bahama Swallow**/Golondrina de Bahamas/**BAHS**	EN	-	R	-	V	-	P
274.	*Stelgidopteryx serripennis*/**Northern Rough-winged Swallow**/Golondrina de Alas Ásperas/**NRWS**	LC	-	FC	-	T-WR	-	PC
	Stelgidopteryx serripennis serripennis (Northern)	LC	-	FC	-	T-WR	-	PC
	Stelgidopteryx serripennis psammochrous (Northern)[32]	LC	-	XR	-	V	-	P
275.	*Progne subis subis*/**Purple Martin (subis/arboricola)**/Golondrina Azul Americana/**PUMA**	LC	-	FC	-	T	-	QC
276.	*Progne cryptoleuca*/**Cuban Martin**/Golondrina Azul Cubana/**CUMA**	LC	-	Co	Br	SR	-	PC
277.	*Progne dominicensis*/**Caribbean Martin**/Golondrina Caribeña/**CAMA**	LC	-	VR	Br[33]	V	-	P
278.	*Hirundo rustica erythrogaster*/**Barn Swallow (American)**/Golondrina Cola de Tijera/**BARS**	LC	-	Co	-	T-WR	-	PC
279.	*Petrochelidon pyrrhonota pyrrhonota*/**Cliff Swallow (pyrrhonota Group)**/Golondrina de Farallón/**CLSW**	LC	-	R-U?	-	T	-	P
280.	*Petrochelidon fulva fulva*/**Cave Swallow (Caribbean)**/Golondrina de Cuevas/**CASW**	LC	-	Co	Br	T-SR[PM]	-	PC
	1.44. KINGLETS, WAXWINGS, GNATCATCHERS AND WRENS							
	Order: PASSERIFORMES Family: Regulidae							
281.	*Corthylio calendula calendula*/**Ruby-crowned Kinglet**/Reyezuelo/**RCKI**	LC	-	R	-	V-WR?	-	P
	Order: PASSERIFORMES Family: Bombycillidae							
282.	*Bombycilla garrulus* (prob. *pallidiceps*)/**Bohemian Waxwing**/Picotero Europeo/**BOWA**[34]	LC	-	VR	-	V	-	P

	English Name/Cuban Common Name (CCN)/*Latin Name*/Alpha Code	Threat status	End. Reg.	Abun. status	Breed status	Resid. status	Ext.	Dist.
283.	*Bombycilla cedrorum*/**Cedar Waxwing**/Picotero del Cedro/**CEDW**	LC	-	U	-	T-WR	-	P
	Order: PASSERIFORMES Family: Polioptilidae							
284.	*Polioptila lembeyei*/**Cuban Gnatcatcher**/Sinsontillo/**CUGN**	LC	CU	FC	Br	YR	-	Rg
285.	*Polioptila caerulea caerulea*/**Blue-gray Gnatcatcher**/Rabudita/**BGGN**	LC	-	Co	-	T-WR	-	PC
	Order: PASSERIFORMES Family: Troglodytidae							
286.	*Troglodytes aedon aedon*/**House Wren (Northern)**/Troglodita Americano/**HOWR**[35]	LC	-	VR	-	V	-	P
287.	*Ferminia cerverai*/**Zapata Wren**/Ferminia/**ZAWR**[36]	EN	CU	U	Br	YR	-	L
	Order: PASSERIFORMES Family: Mimidae							
288.	*Dumetella carolinensis*/**Gray Catbird**/Zorzal Gato/**GRCA**	LC	-	Co	-	T-WR	-	PC
289.	*Toxostoma rufum rufum*/**Brown Thrasher**/Sinsonte Colorado/**BRTH**	LC	-	VR	-	V	-	P
290.	*Mimus gundlachii*/**Bahama Mockingbird**/Sinsonte Prieto/**BAMO**[37]	LC	GA-LY	R	Br	YR	-	L
	Mimus gundlachii gundlachii	NT	CU-LY	R	Br	YR	-	L
291.	*Mimus polyglottos orpheus*/**Northern Mockingbird**/Sinsonte/**NOMO**	LC	-	Co	Br	YR	-	PC
	Order: PASSERIFORMES Family: Sturnidae							
292.	*Sturnus vulgaris vulgaris*/**European Starling**/Estornino/**EUST**	LC	-	VR	-	V	-	P
293.	*Acridotheres tristis*/**Common Myna**/Miná Común/**COMY**	LC	-	VR	Br	V	P-C6	P
	1.45. SOLITAIRES, THRUSHES AND MIMICS							
	Order: PASSERIFORMES Family: Turdidae							
294.	*Sialia sialis sialis*/**Eastern Bluebird (Eastern)**/Azulejo Pechirrojo/**EABL**	LC	-	R	-	T-WR	-	P
295.	*Myadestes elisabeth*/**Cuban Solitaire**/Ruiseñor/**CUSO**	NT/*VU*	CU	FC	Br	YR	-	L
	Myadestes elisabeth elisabeth	NT/*VU*	CU	FC	Br	YR	-	L
	Myadestes elisabeth retrusus	Ex	CU	†	Br	YR	-	L
296.	*Catharus fuscescens*/**Veery**/Tordo Colorado/**VEER**	LC	-	R	-	T	-	P
	Catharus fuscescens fuscescens	LC	-	R	-	T	-	P
	Catharus fuscescens salicicola	LC	-	VR?	-	T	-	P
297.	*Catharus minimus*/**Gray-cheeked Thrush**/Tordo de Mejillas Grises/**GCTH**	LC	-	U	-	T	-	L
	Catharus minimus minimus	LC	-	U	-	T	-	P
	Catharus minimus aliciae	LC	-	U	-	T	-	L
298.	*Catharus bicknelli*/**Bicknell's Thrush**/Tordo de Bicknell/**BITH**	VU/*EN*	-	U	-	T-WR	-	L
299.	*Catharus ustulatus* prob. *swainsoni*/**Swainson's Thrush (Olive-backed)**/Tordo de Espalda Olivada/**SWTH**	LC	-	FC	-	T-WR	-	L

English Name/Cuban Common Name (CCN)/*Latin Name*/Alpha Code		Threat status	End. Reg.	Abun. status	Breed status	Resid. status	Ext.	Dist.
300.	*Catharus guttatus* (prob. *faxoni*)/**Hermit Thrush**/Tordo de Cola Colorada/**HETH**	LC	-	VR	-	V	-	P
301.	*Hylocichla mustelina*/**Wood Thrush**/Tordo Pecoso/**WOTH**	LC	-	R	-	T-WR	-	P
302.	*Turdus migratorius*/**American Robin (migratorius Group)**/Zorzal Migratorio/**AMRO**	LC	-	R	-	T	-	P
	Turdus migratorius migratorius (*migratorius* Group)	LC	-	R	-	T-WR?	-	P
	Turdus migratorius achrusterus (*migratorius* Group)	LC	-	VR	-	V?	-	P
303.	*Turdus plumbeus*/**Red-legged Thrush**/Zorzal Real/**RLTH**	LC	CU-GA-WC	Co	Br	YR	-	PC
	Turdus plumbeus schistaceus (*rubripes* Group)	LC	CU	Co	Br	YR	-	Rg
	Turdus plumbeus rubripes (*rubripes* Group)	LC	CU	Co	Br	YR	-	QC
1.46. FINCHES AND SPARROWS								
Order: PASSERIFORMES Family: Estrildidae								
304.	*Lonchura punctulata* ssp./**Scaly-breasted Munia (Checkered)**/Damero/**SBMU**	LC	-	FC	Br	YR	N-C1-C5?	PC
305.	*Lonchura malacca* ssp./**Tricolored Munia**/Monjita Tricolor/**TRMU**	LC	-	FC	Br	YR	N-C1-C5?	PC
306.	**Lonchura atricapilla* ssp./**Chestnut Munia**/Monjita Castaña/**CHMU**	LC	-	R	Br	YR	N-C1-C5?	L
Order: PASSERIFORMES Family: Muscicapidae								
307.	*Oenanthe oenanthe* prob. *leucorhoa*/**Northern Wheatear (Greenland)**/Tordo del Ártico/**NOWH**[38]	LC	-	VR	-	V	-	P
Order: PASSERIFORMES Family: Passeridae								
308.	*Passer domesticus domesticus*/**House Sparrow**/Gorrión Doméstico/**HOSP**	LC	-	Co	Br	YR	N-C1	PC
Order: PASSERIFORMES Family: Motacillidae								
309.	*Anthus rubescens rubescens*/**American Pipit (rubescens Group)**/Bisbita Norteamericana (SEO)/**AMPI**	LC	-	VR	-	V-WR?	-	P
Order: PASSERIFORMES Family: Fringillidae								
310.	*Spinus psaltria jouyi*/**Lesser Goldfinch**/Chichí Bacal/**LEGO**	LC	-	-	-	-	P-C6	L
311.	**Spinus tristis* sp. (prob. *tristis*)/**American Goldfinch**/Jilguero Americano[39]/**AMGO**	LC	-	VR	-	V	-	P
Order: PASSERIFORMES Family: Calcariidae								
312.	*Calcarius lapponicus lapponicus*/**Lapland Longspur**/Escribano Lapón (SEO)/**LALO**[40]	LC	-	VR	-	V	-	P
Order: PASSERIFORMES Family: Passerellidae								
313.	*Ammodramus savannarum pratensis*/**Grasshopper Sparrow**/Chamberguito/**GRSP**	LC	-	U	-	T-WR	-	QC
314.	*Chondestes grammacus grammacus*/**Lark Sparrow**/Gorrión de Uñas Largas /**LASP**	LC	-	R-VR	-	T-WR?	-	P

	English Name/Cuban Common Name (CCN)/*Latin Name*/Alpha Code	Threat status	End. Reg.	Abun. status	Breed status	Resid. status	Ext.	Dist.
315.	*Spizella passerina passerina*/**Chipping Sparrow**/Gorrión de Cabeza Parda/**CHSP**	LC	-	R	-	V-WR?	-	P
316.	*Spizella pallida*/**Clay-colored Sparrow**/Gorrión Colorado/**CCSP**	LC	-	U-R	-	T-WR	-	P
317.	*Junco hyemalis*/**Dark-eyed Junco**/Junco de Ojos Oscuros/**DEJU**	LC	-	VR	-	V	-	P
	Junco hyemalis hyemalis/**SCJU**/(Slate-colored)[41]	LC	-	VR	-	V	-	P
	Junco hyemalis mearnsi/**PSJU**/(Pink-sided)	LC	-	VR	-	V	-	P
318.	*Zonotrichia leucophrys*/**White-crowned Sparrow**/Gorrión de Coronilla Blanca/**WCSP**	LC	-	U-R	-	T-WR	-	P
	Zonotrichia leucophrys leucophrys/**EWCS**/(leucophrys)	LC	-	U	-	T-WR?	-	P
	Zonotrichia leucophrys gambelii/**GWCS**/(Gambel's)	LC	-	U	-	T-WR	-	P
319.	*Zonotrichia querula*/**Harris's Sparrow**/Gorrión de Harris/	NT	-	VR	-	V	-	P
320.	*Zonotrichia albicollis* (white striped morph)/**White-throated Sparrow**/Gorrión de Garganta Blanca/**WTSP**	LC	-	VR	-	V	-	P
321.	*Passerculus sandwichensis sandwichensis*/**Savannah Sparrow (Savannah)**/Gorrión de Sabana/**SAVS**	LC	-	U	-	T-WR	-	QC
322.	*Melospiza lincolnii lincolnii*/**Lincoln's Sparrow**/Gorrión de Lincoln/**LISP**	LC	-	U	-	T-WR?	-	QC
323.	*Melospiza melodia*/**Song Sparrow**/Gorrión Cantor/**SOSP**[42]	LC	-	VR	-	V	-	P
324.	*Torreornis inexpectata*/**Zapata Sparrow**/Cabrerito de la Ciénaga/**ZASP**	VU/*EN*	CU	U	Br	YR	-	L
	Torreornis inexpectata inexpectata	VU/*EN*	CU	U	Br	YR	-	L
	Torreornis inexpectata sigmani	EN	CU	U	Br	YR	-	L
	Torreornis inexpectata varonai	EN	CU	U	Br	YR	-	L
325.	*Pipilo chlorurus*/**Green-tailed Towhee**/Gorrión de Cola Verde/**GTTO**	LC	-	VR	-	V	-	P
	**1.47. SPINDALIS, BLACKBIRDS, ORIOLES AND ALLIES**
	Order: PASSERIFORMES Family: Spindalidae
326.	*Spindalis zena*/**Western Spindalis**/Cabrero/**WESP**	LC	GA-LY-WC	Co	Br	YR	-	PC
	Spindalis zena pretrei[43]	LC	CU	Co	Br	YR	-	PC
	Order: PASSERIFORMES Family: Teretistridae
327.	*Teretistris fernandinae*/**Yellow-headed Warbler**/Chillina/**YHWA**	LC	CU	Co	Br	YR	-	Rg
328.	*Teretistris fornsi*/**Oriente Warbler**/Pechero/**ORWA**	LC	CU	Co	Br	YR	-	Rg
	Order: PASSERIFORMES Family: Icteriidae
329.	*Icteria virens virens*/**Yellow-breasted Chat (virens)**/Bijirita Grande/**YBCH**	LC	-	R	-	T-WR?	-	P

	English Name/Cuban Common Name (CCN)/*Latin Name*/Alpha Code	Threat status	End. Reg.	Abun. status	Breed status	Resid. status	Ext.	Dist.
	Order: PASSERIFORMES Family: Icteridae							
330.	*Xanthocephalus xanthocephalus*/**Yellow-headed Blackbird**/Mayito de Cabeza Amarilla/**YHBL**[44]	LC	-	VR	-	V	-	P
331.	*Dolichonyx oryzivorus*/**Bobolink**/Chambergo/**BOBO**	LC	-	FC-R	-	T	-	L
332.	*Sturnella magna*/**Eastern Meadowlark**/Sabanero/**EAME**	NT	-	Co	Br	YR	-	PC
	Sturnella magna hippocrepis/**Eastern Meadowlark (Cuban)**/*Sabanero*	LC	CU	Co	Br	YR	-	PC
333.	*Icterus melanopsis*/**Cuban Oriole**/Solibio/**CUOR**	LC	CU	Co	Br	YR	-	PC
334.	*Icterus spurius*/**Orchard Oriole (Orchard)**/Turpial de Huertos/**OROR**	LC	-	U-R	-	T-WR[45]	-	P
335.	*Icterus cucullatus* (cf. *igneus*)/**Hooded Oriole**/Turpial de Capucha/**HOOR**	LC	-	XR	-	V	-	P
336.	*Icterus galbula*/**Baltimore Oriole**/Turpial/**BAOR**	LC	-	FC	-	T-WR	-	PC
337.	*Agelaius assimilis*/**Red-shouldered Blackbird**/Mayito de Ciénaga/**RSBL**	LC/*VU*	CU	FC	Br	YR	-	L
338.	*Agelaius humeralis*/**Tawny-shouldered Blackbird**/Mayito/**TSBL**	LC	GA	FC	Br	YR	-	PC
	Agelaius humeralis scopulus	LC	CU	FC	Br	YR	-	L
	Agelaius humeralis humeralis	LC	GA	FC	Br	YR	-	PC
339.	*Molothrus bonariensis minimus*/**Shiny Cowbird**/Pájaro Vaquero/**SHCO**	LC	-	Co	Br	YR	-	PC
340.	*Molothrus ater ater*/**Brown-headed Cowbird**/Pajaro Vaquero Americano/**BHCO**[46]	LC	-	R	-	V	-	P
341.	*Ptiloxena atroviolacea*/**Cuban Blackbird**/Totí/**CUBL**	LC	CU	Co	Br	YR	-	PC
342.	*Quiscalus mexicanus*/**Great-tailed Grackle**/Chichinguaco Mexicano/**GTGR**[47]	LC	-	VR	-	V	-	P
343.	*Quiscalus niger*/**Greater Antillean Grackle**/Chichinguaco/**GAGR**	LC	GA	Co	Br	YR	-	PC
	Quiscalus niger caribaeus	LC	CU	Co	Br	YR	-	Rg
	Quiscalus niger gundlachii	LC	CU	Co	Br	YR	-	QC
	1.48. WARBLERS							
	Order: PASSERIFORMES Family: Parulidae							
344.	*Seiurus aurocapilla*/**Ovenbird**/Señorita de Monte/**OVEN**	LC	-	Co	-	T-WR	-	PC
	Seiurus aurocapilla aurocapilla	LC	-	Co	-	T-WR	-	PC
	Seiurus aurocapilla furvior	LC	-	VR	-	V	-	P
345.	*Helmitheros vermivorum*/**Worm-eating Warbler**/Bijirita Gusanera/**WEWA**	LC	-	FC	-	T-WR	-	PC
346.	*Parkesia motacilla*/**Louisiana Waterthrush**/Señorita de Río/**LOWA**	LC	-	Co	-	T-WR	-	PC

	English Name/Cuban Common Name (CCN)/*Latin Name*/Alpha Code	Threat status	End. Reg.	Abun. status	Breed status	Resid. status	Ext.	Dist.
347.	*Parkesia noveboracensis*/**Northern Waterthrush**/Señorita de Manglar/**NOWA**	LC	-	Co	-	T-WR	-	PC
348.	*Vermivora bachmanii*/**Bachman's Warbler**/Bijirita de Bachman/**BAWA**	CR (PE)	-	†?	-	WR	-	L
349.	*Vermivora chrysoptera*/**Golden-winged Warbler**/Bijirita de Alas Doradas/**GWWA**	NT	-	R	-	T	-	P
350.	*Vermivora cyanoptera*/**Blue-winged Warbler**/Bijirita de Alas Azules/**BWWA**	LC	-	R	-	T-WR	-	P
351.	*Mniotilta varia*/**Black-and-white Warbler**/Bijirita Trepadora/**BAWW**	LC	-	Co	-	T-WR	-	PC
352.	*Protonotaria citrea*/**Prothonotary Warbler**/Bijirita Protonotaria/**PROW**	LC	-	FC	-	T-WR	-	PC
353.	*Limnothlypis swainsonii*/**Swainson's Warbler**/Bijirita de Swainson/**SWWA**	LC	-	U	-	T-WR	-	PC
354.	*Leiothlypis peregrina*/**Tennessee Warbler**/Bijirita de Tennessee/**TEWA**	LC	-	FC	-	T-WR	-	L
355.	*Leiothlypis celata celata*/**Orange-crowned Warbler (celata)**/Bijirita de Coronilla Anaranjada/**OCWA**	LC	-	R	-	V-WR?	-	P
356.	*Leiothlypis ruficapilla ruficapilla*/**Nashville Warbler (ruficapilla)**/Bijirita de Nashville/**NAWA**	LC	-	R	-	V-WR?	-	P
357.	*Oporornis agilis*/**Connecticut Warbler**/Bijirita de Connecticut/**CONW**[48]	LC	-	R	-	V	-	P
358.	*Geothlypis philadelphia*/**Mourning Warbler**/Bijirita de Cabeza Gris/**MOWA**	LC	-	VR	-	V	-	P
359.	*Geothlypis formosa*/**Kentucky Warbler**/Bijirita de Kentucky/**KEWA**	LC	-	R	-	T-WR	-	P
360.	*Geothlypis trichas trichas*/**Common Yellowthroat (trichas Group)**/Caretica/**COYE**	LC	-	Co	-	T-WR	-	PC
361.	*Setophaga citrina*/**Hooded Warbler**/Monjita/**HOYE**	LC	-	U	-	T-WR	-	PC
362.	*Setophaga ruticilla*/**American Redstart**/Candelita/**AMRE**	LC	-	Co	-	WR[PM]	-	PC
363.	*Setophaga kirtlandii*/**Kirtland's Warbler**/Bijirita de Kirtland/**KIWA**	NT	-	XR	-	V	-	P
364.	*Setophaga tigrina*/**Cape May Warbler**/Bijirita Atigrada/**CMWA**	LC	-	Co	-	T-WR	-	PC
365.	*Setophaga cerulea*/**Cerulean Warbler**/Bijirita Azulosa/**CERW**	NT	-	R	-	T	-	P
366.	*Setophaga americana*/**Northern Parula**/Bijirita Chica/**NOPA**	LC	-	Co	-	T-WR	-	PC
367.	*Setophaga magnolia*/**Magnolia Warbler**/Bijirita Magnolia/**MAWA**	LC	-	Co	-	T-WR	-	PC
368.	*Setophaga castanea*/**Bay-breasted Warbler**/Bijirita Castaña/**BBWA**	LC	-	R	-	T	-	QC
369.	*Setophaga fusca*/**Blackburnian Warbler**/Bijirita Blackburniana/**BLBW**	LC	-	R	-	T	-	P

	English Name/Cuban Common Name (CCN)/*Latin Name*/Alpha Code	Threat status	End. Reg.	Abun. status	Breed status	Resid. status	Ext.	Dist.
370.	☐ *Setophaga petechia*/**Yellow Warbler**/Canario de Manglar/**YEWA**[49]	LC	-	Co	Br	T-YR	-	P
	☐ *Setophaga petechia aestiva* (**Northern**)	LC	-	FC	-	T	-	P
	☐ *Setophaga petechia gundlachi* (**Golden**)	LC	-	Co	Br	YR	-	PC
371.	☐ *Setophaga pensylvanica*/**Chestnut-sided Warbler**/Bijirita de Costados Castaños/**CSWA**	LC	-	U	-	T	-	QC
372.	☐ *Setophaga striata*/**Blackpoll Warbler**/Bijirita de Cabeza Negra/**BLPW**	NT	-	FC	-	T-WR?	-	QC
373.	☐ *Setophaga caerulescens*/**Black-throated Blue Warbler**/Bijirita Azul de Garganta Negra/**BTBW**	LC	-	Co	-	T-WR	-	PC
	☐ *Setophaga caerulescens caerulescens*	LC	-	Co	-	T-WR	-	PC
	☐ *Setophaga caerulescens cairnsi*	LC	-	U	-	T-WR	-	QC
374.	☐ *Setophaga palmarum*/**Palm Warbler**/Bijirita Común/**PAWA**	LC	-	Co	-	T-WR	-	PC
	☐ *Setophaga palmarum palmarum*/**WPWA**/(**Western**)	LC	-	Co	-	T-WR	-	PC
	☐ *Setophaga palmarum hypochrysea*/**YPWA**/(**Yellow**)	LC	-	R	-	T-WR?	-	P
375.	☐ *Setophaga pityophila*/**Olive-capped Warbler**/Bijirita del Pinar/**OCAW**	LC/*VU*	CU-LY	Co	Br	YR	-	Rg
376.	☐ *Setophaga pinus pinus*/**Pine Warbler**/Bijirita de Pinos/**PIWA**	LC	-	R	-	T	-	P
377.	☐ *Setophaga coronata*/**Yellow-rumped Warbler**/Bijirita Coronada/**YRWA**	LC	-	FC	-	T-WR	-	PC
	☐ *Setophaga coronata coronata*/**MYWA**/(**Myrtle**)	LC	-	FC	-	T-WR	-	PC
	☐ *Setophaga coronata auduboni*/**AUWA**/(**Audubon's**)[50]	LC	-	VR	-	V	-	P
378.	☐ *Setophaga dominica*/**Yellow-throated Warbler**/Bijirita de Garganta Amarilla/**YTWA**	LC	-	Co	-	T-WR	-	PC
	☐ *Setophaga dominica dominica* (dominica/stoddardi)	LC	-	Co	-	T-WR	-	PC
	☐ *Setophaga dominica stoddardi* (dominica/stoddardi)	LC	-	R	-	T-WR?	-	P
	☐ *Setophaga dominica albilora* (albilora)	LC	-	Co	-	T-WR	-	PC
379.	☐ *Setophaga discolor*/**Prairie Warbler**/Mariposa Galana/**PRAW**	LC	-	Co	-	T-WR	-	PC
	☐ *Setophaga discolor discolor*	LC	-	Co	-	T-WR	-	PC
	☐ *Setophaga discolor paludicola*	LC	-	R	-	T-WR	-	P
380.	☐ *Setophaga nigrescens* ssp./**Black-throated Gray Warbler**/Bijirita Gris/**BTYW**	LC	-	XR	-	V	-	P
381.	☐ *Setophaga townsendi*/**Townsend's Warbler**/Bijirita de Townsend/**TOWA**[51]	LC	-	XR	-	V	-	P
382.	☐ *Setophaga virens*/**Black-throated Green Warbler**/Bijirita de Garganta Negra/**BTNW**	LC	-	Co	-	T-WR	-	PC

	English Name/Cuban Common Name (CCN)/*Latin Name*/Alpha Code	Threat status	End. Reg.	Abun. status	Breed status	Resid. status	Ext.	Dist.
383.	*Cardellina canadensis*/**Canada Warbler**/Bijirita de Canadá/**CAWA**	LC	-	VR	-	T-WR	-	P
384.	*Cardellina pusilla pileolata*/**Wilson's Warbler**/Bijirita de Wilson/**WIWA**	LC	-	R	-	T-WR	-	P
	Cardellina pusilla pileolata (pileolata)	LC	-	VR	-	T-WR	-	P
	Cardellina pusilla pusilla (pusilla)	LC	-	R	-	T	-	P

1.49. TANAGERS, GROSSBEAKS, BUNTINGS AND ALLIES
Order: PASSERIFORMES   Family: Cardinalidae

385.	*Piranga rubra rubra*/**Summer Tanager**/Cardenal Rojo/**SUTA**	LC	-	FC	-	T-WR	-	QC
386.	*Piranga olivacea*/**Scarlet Tanager**/Cardenal Alinegro/**SCTA**	LC	-	U	-	T	-	PC
387.	*Piranga ludoviciana*/**Western Tanager**/Cardenal del Oeste/**WETA**[52]	LC	-	VR	-	V	-	P
388.	*Pheucticus ludovicianus*/**Rose-breasted Grosbeak**/Degollado/**RBGR**	LC	-	FC	-	T-WR	-	PC
389.	*Pheucticus melanocephalus*/**Black-headed Grosbeak**/Degollado Cabecinregro[53]/**BHGR**	LC	-	XR	-	V	-	P
390.	*Passerina caerulea caerulea*/**Blue Grosbeak**/Azulejón/**BLGR**	LC	-	FC	-	T-WR	-	PC
391.	*Passerina amoena*/**Lazuli Bunting**/Mariposa Azul/**LAZB**	LC	-	VR	-	V-T?	-	P
392.	*Passerina cyanea*/**Indigo Bunting**/Azulejo/**INBU**	LC	-	FC	-	T-WR	-	PC
393.	*Passerina ciris ciris*/**Painted Bunting**/Mariposa/**PABU**	LC/*VU*	-	U	-	T-WR	-	PC
394.	*Spiza americana*/**Dickcissel**/Gorrión de Pecho Amarillo/**DICK**	LC	-	R	-	T	-	P

Order: PASSERIFORMES   Family: Thraupidae

395.	*Sicalis flaveola ssp.*/**Saffron Finch (Saffron)**/Gorrión Azafrán/**SAFI**	LC	-	VR	-	V	N-C5?	P
396.	**Volatinia jacarina splendens*/**Blue-black Grassquit**/Arrocero Negrito/**BGRA**[54]	LC	-	XR	-	V	?	P
397.	*Cyanerpes cyaneus carneipes*/**Red-legged Honeycreeper**/Aparecido de San Diego/**RLHO**	LC	-	Co	Br	YR	-[55]	PC
398.	*Coereba flaveola bahamensis*/**Bananaquit (Bahamas)**/Reinita/**BANA**	LC	-	R	-?	V- YR?	-	L
399.	*Tiaris olivaceus olivaceus*/**Yellow-faced Grassquit**/Tomeguín de la Tierra/**YFGR**	LC	-	Co	Br	YR	-	PC
400.	*Melopyrrha nigra*/**Cuban Bullfinch**/Negrito/**CUBU** (see p.12)	NT	CU	FC	Br	YR	-	PC
401.	*Phonipara canora*/**Cuban Grassquit**/Tomeguín del Pinar/**CUGR**	LC	CU	FC	Br	YR	-	PC
402.	*Melanospiza bicolor bicolor*/**Black-faced Grassquit**/Tomeguín Prieto/**BFGR**	LC	-	R	Br	YR	-	P

1.50. Table 2: Cuban Endemisms according to categories

No.	CUBAN ENDEMISMS ACCORDING TO CATEGORIES
	FAMILY LEVEL
1.	Teretistridae
	GENUS LEVEL
1.	*Starnoenas*
2.	*Cyanolimnas*
3.	*Margarobyas*
4.	*Xiphidiopicus*
5.	*Ferminia*
6.	*Torreornis*
7.	*Teretistris*
8.	*Ptiloxena*
9.	*Phonipara*
	SPECIES LEVEL
1.	*Starnoenas cyanocephala*/**Blue-headed Quail-Dove**/Paloma Perdiz
2.	*Geotrygon caniceps*/**Gray-fronted Quail-Dove**/Camao
3.	*Antrostomus cubanensis*/**Cuban Nightjar**/Guabairo
4.	*Mellisuga helenae*/**Bee Hummingbird**/Zunzuncito
5.	*Cyanolimnas cerverai*/**Zapata Rail**/Gallinuela de Santo Tomás
6.	*Chondrohierax wilsonii*/**Cuban Kite**/Gavilán Caguarero
7.	*Accipiter gundlachi*/**Gundlach's Hawk**/Gavilán Colilargo
8.	*Buteogallus gundlachii*/**Cuban Black Hawk**/Gavilán Batista
9.	*Margarobyas lawrencii*/**Bare-legged Owl**/Sijú Cotunto
10.	*Glaucidium sijú*/**Cuban Pygmy-Owl**/Sijú Platanero
11.	*Priotelus temnurus*/**Cuban Trogon**/Tocororo
12.	*Todus multicolor* /**Cuban Tody**/Cartacuba
13.	*Xiphidiopicus percussus* /**Cuban Green Woodpecker**/Carpintero Verde
14.	*Colaptes fernandinae*/**Fernandina's Flicker**/Carpintero Churroso
15.	*Ara tricolor*/**Cuban Macaw**/Guacamayo Cubano †
16.	*Psittacara euops*/**Cuban Parakeet**/Catey
17.	*Vireo gundlachii*/**Cuban Vireo**/Juan Chiví
18.	*Polioptila lembeyei*/**Cuban Gnatcatcher**/Sinsontillo
19.	*Ferminia cerverai*/**Zapata Wren**/Ferminia
20.	*Myadestes elisabeth*/**Cuban Solitaire**/Ruiseñor
21.	*Torreornis inexpectata*/**Zapata Sparrow**/Cabrerito de la Ciénaga
22.	*Teretistris fernandinae*/**Yellow-headed Warbler**/Chillina
23.	*Teretistris fornsi*/**Oriente Warbler** /Pechero
24.	*Icterus melanopsis*/**Cuban Oriole**/Solibio
25.	*Agelaius assimilis*/**Red-shouldered Blackbird**/Mayito de Ciénaga
26.	*Ptiloxena atroviolacea*/**Cuban Blackbird**/Totí
27.	*Phonipara canora*/**Cuban Grassquit**/Tomeguín del Pinar
28.	*Melopyrrha nigra*/**Cuban Bullfinch**/Negrito
	SUBSPECIES LEVEL
1.	*Colinus virginianus cubanensis*/**Northern Bobwhite (Eastern)**/Codorniz
2.	*Coccyzus merlini merlini*/**Great Lizard-Cuckoo (Cuban)**/Arriero o Guacaica
3.	*Coccyzus merlini santamariae*
4.	*Coccyzus merlini decolor*
5.	*Tachornis phoenicobia iradii*/**Antillean Palm-Swift**/Vencejito de Palma
6.	*Rallus elegans ramsdeni*/**King Rail (Northern)**/Gallinuela de Agua Dulce

7.	*Antigone canadensis nesiotes*/**Sandhill Crane (nesiotes)**/Grulla	
8.	*Accipiter striatus fringilloides*/**Sharp-shinned Hawk (Northern)**/Gavilancito	
9.	*Buteo platypterus cubanensis*/**Broad-winged Hawk (Northern)**/Gavilán Bobo	
10.	*Athene cunicularia guantanamensis* /**Burrowing Owl (Florida)**/Sijú de Sabana	
11.	*Asio stygius siguapa*/**Stygian Owl**/Siguapa	
12.	*Melanerpes superciliaris superciliaris*/**West Indian Woodpecker**/Carpintero Jabado	
13.	*Melanerpes superciliaris murceus*	
14.	*Campephilus principalis bairdii*/**Ivory-billed Woodpecker (Cuban)**/Carpintero Real	
15.	*Colaptes auratus chrysocaulosus*/**Northern Flicker (Cuban)**/Carpintero Escapulario	
16.	*Amazona leucocephala leucocephala*/**Cuban Parrot (Cuban)**/Cotorra	
17.	*Tyrannus caudifasciatus caudifasciatus*/**Loggerhead Kingbird (Loggerhead)**/Pitirre Guatíbere	
18.	*Contopus caribaeus caribaeus*/**Cuban Pewee**/Bobito Chico	
19.	*Contopus caribaeus morenoi*	
20.	*Contopus caribaeus nerlyi*	
21.	*Vireo crassirostris cubensis*/**Thick-billed Vireo**/Vireo de Bahamas	
22.	*Turdus plumbeus schistaceus*/**Red-legged Thrush (rubripes Group)**/Zorzal Real	
23.	*Turdus plumbeus rubripes* **(rubripes Group)**	
24.	*Spindalis zena pretrei* /**Western Spindalis**/Cabrero	
25.	*Sturnella magna hippocrepis*/**Eastern Meadowlark (Cuban)**/Sabanero	
26.	*Agelaius humeralis scopulus*/**Tawny-shouldered Blackbird**/Mayito	
27.	*Agelaius humeralis humeralis*	
28.	*Quiscalus niger caribaeus*/**Greater Antillean Grackle**/Chichinguaco	
29.	*Quiscalus niger gundlachii*	
	CARIBBEAN ENDEMICS IN CUBA	**Near Endemic (NE)***
1.	*Dendrocygna arborea*/**West Indian Whistling-Duck**/Yaguasa Cubana	-
2.	*Patagioenas inornata inornata*/**Plain Pigeon**/Torcaza Boba	-
3.	*Coccyzus merlini*/**Great Lizard-Cuckoo**/Arriero o Guacaica	NE
4.	*Tachornis phoenicobia*/**Antillean Palm-Swift**/Vencejito de Palma	-
5.	*Riccordia ricordii*/**Cuban Emerald**/Zunzún	NE
6.	*Melanerpes superciliaris*/**West Indian Woodpecker**/Carpintero Jabado	-
7.	*Amazona leucocephala*/**Cuban Parrot**/Cotorra	-
8.	*Myiarchus sagrae*/**La Sagra's Flycatcher**/Bobito Grande	NE
9.	*Tyrannus caudifasciatus*/**Loggerhead Kingbird**/Pitirre Guatíbere	-
10.	*Tyrannus cubensis*/**Giant Kingbird**/Pitirre Real	NE
11.	*Contopus caribaeus*/**Cuban Pewee**/Bobito Chico	NE
12.	*Vireo crassirostris*/**Thick-billed Vireo**/Vireo de Bahamas	-
13.	*Corvus palmarum*/**Palm Crow**/Cao Pinalero	-
14.	*Corvus nasicus*/**Cuban Crow**/Cao Montero	NE
15.	*Mimus gundlachii*/**Bahama Mockingbird**/Sinsonte Prieto	-
16.	*Turdus plumbeus*/**Red-legged Thrush**/Zorzal Real	-
17.	*Spindalis zena*/**Western Spindalis**/Cabrero	NE
18.	*Agelaius humeralis*/**Tawny-shouldered Blackbird**/Mayito	NE
19.	*Quiscalus niger*/**Greater Antillean Grackle**/Chichinguaco	-
20.	*Setophaga pityophila*/**Olive-capped Warbler**/Bijirita del Pinar	NE

*** Near Endemic (NE):** Considered as an informal status, those species with their largest area of distribution in Cuba, but, in addition, inhabit only another small island or a reduced group of them.

1.51. Table 3: Exotics and unsuccessful introduced species, uncertain origin records

(These birds should not be considered part of the Cuban avifauna and are not included in the main list)

Species or subspecies recorded as unsuccessful introductions, human-assisted transportees or escapees from captivity*, and whose breeding populations (if any) are thought not to be self-sustaining according to the history of Cuban ornithology. For basic information about each species see previous editions of this checklist.

	English Name/Cuban Common Name (CCN)/ *Latin Name*	Refer.	Geog. Cob.	Categ.
	Order: TINAMIFORMES Family: Tinamidae			
1.	☐ *Tinamidae sp. (not specified)*/**Tinamou**	Bond, 1950	Central & South Am.	P-C6
	Order: GALLIFORMES Family: Cracidae			
2.	☐ *Ortalis vetula ssp.*/**Plain Chachalaca**/Chachalaca norteña	Bond, 1950	Central Am.	P-C6
	Order: GALLIFORMES Family: Odontophoridae			
3.	☐ *Callipepla californica ssp.* /**California Quail**/Colín de California (SEO)	Bond, 1950	North & Central Am.	P-C6
4.	☐ *Cyrtonyx montezumae ssp.*/**Montezuma Quail**/Colín de Montezuma	Bond 1950	North & Central Am.	P-C6
	Order: GALLIFORMES Family: Phasianidae			
5.	☐ *Alectoris barbara ssp.*/**Barbary Partridge**/Perdiz Moruna (SEO)	Bond 1950	N. Africa	P-C6
6.	☐ *Meleagris ocellata*/**Ocellated Turkey**/Guajolote (Pavo) Ocelado	Bond 1950	Central Am.	P-C6
7.	☐ *Coturnix japonica*/**Common/Japanese Quail**/Codorniz Común	Navarro 2022	Asia	P-C1
	Order: COLUMBIFORMES Family: Columbidae			
8.	☐ *Geopleia cuneata*/**Diamond Dove**/Paloma Diamante	Navarro 2020	Australia	E
9.	☐ *Streptopelia roseogrisea*/African Collared-Dove/Tórtola de Collar Africana[56]	current edition	Africa	E
	Order: GRUIFORMES Family: Rallidae			
10.	☐ *Aramides sp.*/**Wood-Rail (not specified)**/Cotara (SEO) Gallinuela (sin especificar)	Bond 1950	Central & South Am.	P-C6
	Order: CHARADRIIFORMES Family: Burhinidae			
11.	☐ *Burhinus sp.*/**Thick-knee (not specified prob. Double-striped)**/Alcaraván (sin especificar)	Bond 1950	Cf. Central, South Am. & West Indies	P-C6
	Order: CORACIIFORMES Family: Alcedinidae			
12.	☐ *Alcedo atthis ssp.*/**Common Kingfisher (Common)**/Martín Pescador Europeo	Rodríguez et al., 2005	Eurasia & North Africa	E?
	Order: PSITTACIFORMES Family: Psittacidae			
13.	☐ *Nymphicus holandicus*/**Cockatiel**/Cacatillo	Navarro & Reyes 2017	Australia	E
14.	☐ *Melopsittacus undulatus*/**Budgerigar**/Periquito de Australia	Navarro & Reyes 2017	Australia	E

	English Name/Cuban Common Name (CCN)/ *Latin Name*	Refer.	Geog. Cob.	Categ.
	Order: PSITTACIFORMES Family: Psittaculidae			
15.	*Psittacula krameri ssp.*/**Rose-ringed Parakeet**/Cotorra de Kramer (SEO)	Kirwan 2000	Asia & Africa	E
16.	*Agapornis roseicolis ssp.*/**Rosy-faced Lovebird**/Agapornis	Navarro and Reyes, 2017	Africa	E
	Order: PASSERIFORMES Family: Tityridae			
17.	*Pachyramphus polychopterus spp.*/**White-winged Becard**/Mosquero Cabezón de Alas Blancas[57]	Com. by letter in Bond to Garrido, 1987	South and Central América	?
	Order: PASSERIFORMES Family: Corvidae			
18.	*Corvus splendens ssp.*/**House Crow**/Cuervo de la India	Ryall, 2016	Asia, Australia, Indonesia	E
	Order: PASSERIFORMES Family: Silviidae			
19.	*Sylvia atricapilla*/**Eurasian Blackcap**/Curruca Capirotada (SEO)[58]	Navarro and Ordoñez, 2017	Eurasia	V?-E
	Order: PASSERIFORMES Family: Ploceidae			
20.	*Euplectes cf. hordaceus/afer*/**Bishop sp.**/Obispo sp.[59]	Garrido and Wiley, 2010, amended by Navarro, 2019	Africa	N-C5?/E?
21.	*Euplectes macroura macroura*/**Yellow-mantled Widowbird**/Obispo Dorsiamarillo (SEO)[60]	Rodríguez-Castañeda et al 2017	Africa	E
	Order: PASSERIFORMES Family: Estrildidae			
22.	*Stagonopleura guttata*/**Diamond Firetail**/Diamante Moteado	Navarro, 2022a	Australia	E
23.	*Taeniopygia guttata*/**Zebra Finch**/ Diamante Cebra de Timor	Navarro, 2019a	Africa & Australia	E
24.	*Erythrura gouldiae* (domestic)/**Gouldian Finch**/Lady Gould	Navarro and Reyes, 2017	Australia	E
25.	*Lonchura striata ssp.* (domestic)/**White-rumped Munia**/Isabelita	Navarro, 2021a	SE Asia	E
26.	*Padda oryzivora*/**Java Sparrow**/Gorrión de Java	Navarro and Reyes, 2017	Indonesia	E
	Order: PASSERIFORMES Family: Passeridae			
27.	*Passer luteus*/**Sudan Golden Sparrow**/Gorrión Dorado	Garrido and García, 1975	Africa	E?
	Order: PASSERIFORMES Family: Fringillidae			
28.	*Haemorhous mexicanus* (prob. *frontalis*)/**House Finch**/Gorrión Mexicano[61]	Guerra and Sánchez, 2019	North America	E?
29.	*Carduelis carduelis ssp.*/**European Goldfinch**/Jilguero	Gundlach, 1873	Europe	P-C6?
30.	*Spinus cucullatus*/**Red Siskin**/Jilguero Rojo	Gundlach, 1873	South Am.	E?
31.	*Serinus canaria*/**Island Canary**/Canario	Navarro and Reyes, 2017	Canary Islands	E

	English Name/Cuban Common Name (CCN)/ *Latin Name*	Refer.	Geog. Cob.	Categ.
	Order: PASSERIFORMES Family: Passerellidae			
32.	☐ *Zonotricia capensis ssp.*/**Rufous-collared Sparrow**/Chingolo Común (SEO)	Garrido and García, 1975	Central, South America & West Indies	E?
	Order: PASSERIFORMES Family: Thraupidae			
33.	☐ *Paroaria coronata*/**Red-crested Cardinal**/Cardellina crestada	D´Orbigny in La Sagra, 1839	South Am.	E
34.	☐ *Paroaria dominicana*/**Red-cowled Cardinal**/Cardellina dominica (SEO)	D´Orbigny in La Sagra, 1839	South Am.	E
35.	☐ *Sporophila torqueola*/**Cinnamon-rumped Seedeater**/Semillero Torcaz (SEO)	Bond, 1950	Mexico	E?
36.	☐ *Chlorophanes spiza*/**Green Honeycreeper**/Mielerito Verde (SEO)[62]	Cory, 1886	Central and South America	E

* The inclusion of exotic species escaped from captivity in local and regional bird registries has been and continues to be controversial. However, I am of the opinion that no record of an exotic species in feral conditions should be dismissed, especially since the species was evidently detected under these circumstances and could potentially be established at some point, given optimal conditions. The monitoring of these species is of vital importance; through these records (e.g., eBird) we can learn the historical frequency of occurrence, the most represented sites, the tendency of each to be observed, as well as the species involved, taking into account that every country has certain introduced species for use and marketing as exotic pets. All these parameters are important to be able to predict where and how they can be established at a given time and thus facilitate designing appropriate control protocols. It is worth emphasizing that exotic species that have potentially escaped from a cage, as long as they have not established a population, cannot be considered part of the avifauna of a country or be included in its main list.

1.52. Table 4: Unconfirmed Forms

(These should not be considered in any way as part of the Cuban avifauna until official records are confirmed)

Species or subspecies that has been mentioned in different media but with doubtful, uncertain or unsatisfactory confirmation status for the Cuban archipelago. Underlined refers to cases at subspecific level.

	English Name/ Cuban Common Name (CCN)/ *Latin Name*
	Order: ANSERIFORMES Family: Anatidae
1.	☐ *Anas rubripes*/**American Black Duck**/Pato Negro Americano
2.	☐ *Aythya marila neartica*/**Greater Scaup**/Pato Morisco Raro
3.	☐ *Bucephala clangula*/**Common Goldeneye**/Porrón Osculado
4.	☐ *Anas fulvigula fulvigula*/**Mottled Duck**/Pato Moteado
	Order: APODIFORMES Family: Apodidae
5.	☐ *Cypseloides niger <u>borealis</u>*/**Black Swift (borealis)**/Vencejo
	Order: CHARADRIIFORMES Family: Scolopacidae
6.	☐ *Calidris ferruginea*/**Curlew Sandpiper**/Correlimos Zarapitín
7.	☐ *Calidris bairdii*/**Baird´s Sandpiper**/Playerito Unicolor
	Order: CHARADRIIFORMES Family: Scolopacidae
8.	☐ *Egretta gularis*/**Western Reef-Heron**/Garceta Dimorfa
	Order: PASSERIFORMES Family: Troglodytidae
9.	☐ *Cistothorus palustris* ssp./**Marsh Wren**/Troglodita de Ciénaga
	Order: PASSERIFORMES Family: Ploceidae
10.	☐ *Ploceus cucullatus*/**Village Weaver**/Tejedor Común (SEO)[63]
	Order: PASSERIFORMES Family: Fringillidae
11.	☐ *Haemorhous purpureus*/**Purple Finch**/Camachuelo Purpúreo
12.	☐ *Coccothraustes vespertinus*/**Evening Grosbeak**/Picogordo Vespertino (SEO)
13.	☐ *Spinus pinus*/**Pine Siskin**/Jilguero de los Pinos (SEO)
	Order: PASSERIFORMES Family: Icteridae
14.	☐ *Icterus gularis*/**Altamira Oriole**/Turpial de Altamira[64]
15.	☐ *Icterus mesomelas* ssp./**Yellow-tailed Oriole**/Turpial de Cola
16.	☐ *Euphagus carolinus* ssp./**Rusty Blackbird**/Zanate Canadiense
	Order: PASSERIFORMES Family: Parulidae
17.	☐ *Leiothlypis virginiae*/**Virginia's Warbler**/Bijirita de Virginia
	Order: PASSERIFORMES Family: Cardinalidae
18.	☐ *Cardinalis cardinalis* ssp./**Northern Cardinal**/Cardenal
19.	☐ *Passerina rositae*/**Rose-bellied Bunting**/Mariposa de Vientre Rosado[65]
20.	☐ *Passerina ciris <u>pallidior</u>*/**Painted Bunting**/Mariposa

1.53. Table 5: List of Fossil and Extinct Birds of Cuba*

(The information provided is based on Orihuela, 2019, updated by Suarez, 2022)

	Species	Range
	Order: CAPRIMULGIFORMES Family: Caprimulgidae	
1.	*Siphonorhis daiquiri*/**Cuban Pauraque n.c.n.**/Torico Cubano	Cuba
	Order: GRUIFORMES Family: Rallidae	
2.	*Nesotrochis picapicensis*/**Pica-Pica´s Rail**/Gallinuela de Pica Pica	Cuba
	Order: GRUIFORMES Family: Gruidae	
3.	*Antigone cubensis*/**Cuban Flightless Crane**/Grulla Cubana	Cuba
	Order: CHARADRIIFORMES Family: Burhinidae	
4.	*Burhinus bistriatus*/**Double-striped Thick-knee**/Alcaraván Venezolano (Búcaro)	North and Middle America, Greater Antilles, Bahamas, Cuba
	Order: CHARADRIIFORMES Family: Scolopacidae	
5.	*Gallinago kakuki*/**West Indian Snipe**/Becasina Caribeña (Isleña)	Greater Antilles, Cayman Islands, Bahamas, Cuba
	Order: CICONIIFORMES Family: Ciconiidae	
6.	*Ciconia maltha*/**La Brea Stork**/Cigüeña de la Brea	Pan-American
7.	*Ciconia sp.*/**Stork n.c.n.**/Cigueña s.n.c.	Cuba?
8.	*Mycteria wetmorei*/**Wetmore's Stork**/Cayama de Wetmore	North America-Cuba
	Order: PELECANIFORMES Family: Ardeidae	
9.	*Tigrisoma mexicanum*/**Bare-throated Tiger Heron**/Garza Tigre Mexicana[66]	Middle America
	Order: CICONIIFORMES Family: Teratornithidae	
10.	*Oscaravis olsoni*/**Cuban Teratorn**/Teratorno Cubano	Cuba
	Order: CATHARTIFORMES Family: Cathartidae	
11.	*Gymnogyps varonai*/**Cuban Condor**/Cóndor Cubano	Cuba
12.	*Coragyps seductus*/**Cuban Black Vulture**/Zopilote Cubano	Cuba
13.	*Cathartes emsliei*/**Emslie's Vulture**/Aura de Emslie	Cuba
	Order: ACCIPITRIFORMES Family: Accipitridae	
14.	*Gigantohierax suarezi*/**Suárez's Giant Eagle**/Águila Gigante de Suárez	Cuba
15.	*Gigantohierax itchei*/**Itche's Eagle**/Águila de Itche	Cuba
16.	*Buteogallus cf. fragilis*/**Fragile Eagle**/Gavilán Frágil	North America-Cuba
17.	*Buteogallus borrasi*/**Borras' Hawk**/Gavilán de Borrás	Cuba
18.	*Buteogallus royi*/**Roy's Hawk**/Gavilán de Roy	Cuba
19.	*Buteogallus irpus*/**Wolf Hawk**/Gavilán Lobo	Cuba-Hispaniola
20.	*Buteo lineatus*/**Red-shouldered Hawk**/Gavilán de Hombros Rojos	North America- Bahamas-Cuba
21.	*Buteo sanfelipensis*/**San Felipe's Hawk**/Gavilán de San felipe	Cuba
	Order: STRIGIFORMES Family: Tytonidae	
22.	*Tyto pollens*/**Bahamian Giant Barn Owl**/Lechuza Gigante de las Bahamas	Cuba
23.	*Tyto noeli*/ **Noel's Giant Barn Owl**/Lechuza Gigante de Noel	Jamaica, Barbuda, Cuba
24.	*Tyto cravesae*/**Craves's Giant Owl**/Lechuza Gigante de Craves	Cuba

	Species	Range
25.	*Tyto maniola*/**Cuban Dwarf Barn Owl**/Lechuza Enana de Cuba	Cuba
Order: STRIGIFORMES Family: Strigidae		
26.	*Pulsatrix arredondoi*/**Arredondo's Owl**/Búho de Arredondo	Cuba
27.	*Bubo osvaldoi*/**Osvaldo's Owl**/Buho de Osvaldo	Cuba
28.	*Ornimegalonyx oteroi*/**Cuban Giant Owl**/Búho Gigante Cubano	Cuba
29.	*Ornimegalonyx ewingi*/**Ewing's Owl**/Búho de Ewing	Cuba
Order: FALCONIFORMES Family: Falconidae		
30.	*Caracara creightoni*/**Creighton's Caracara**/Caraira de Creighton	Cuba- Bahamas
31.	*Milvago carbo*/**Cuban Caracara**/Caraira Cubana	Cuba
32.	*Milvago diazfrancoi*/**Diaz Franco's Caracara**/Caraira de Díaz Franco	Cuba
33.	*Falco femoralis*/**Aplomado Falcon**/Halcón Aplomado	Southern United States-southern South America
34.	*Falco kurochkini*/**Cuban Flacon**/Halcón Cubano	Cuba
Order: PSITTACIFORMES Family: Psittacidae		
35.	*Ara tricolor*/**Cuban Macaw**/Guacamayo Cubano	Cuba

* The list refers only to birds found in the fossil record that are currently extinct within the range between the Upper Pleistocene and early Holocene. It is important to note that other living species have also been found in the Cuban fossil record; others that are already extinct in recent times have not yet been found as fossils and for this reason they have not been included in this list.

** n.c.n./s.n.c.: No common name

1.54. Comments

1 *Branta bernicla nigricans*/**Brant (Black)**/Ganso Carinegro: This is the first record of this species for Cuba (see section **1.18 New records and reports of Rare Birds**, p. 19), which belongs to the dark form. An individual was recorded during a bird watching tour in one of the ponds in Salinas de Brito, Ciénaga de Zapata, Matanzas province. The record was uploaded to eBird by Robert Lockett (2022), detected and identified by Cynthia Lawes, the accompanying photos (4) were taken by Alejandro Alfonso García (ECOTUR Guide) and Craig Robson. It is a typical species of the arctic zone and shared between North America and Europe. Differentiated into three races, of which the nominal (*bernicla*) is exclusive to northern Europe and the other two are shared and typical of the Atlantic (*hrota*) and Pacific (*nigricans*) coasts. In the Caribbean there are isolated records of this species, which apparently involved the subspecies *hrota* in 1876 in Barbados (Kirwan et al., 2019) and corroborated for *nigricans* in Puerto Rico 1977 and 2009 (Lewis 2009) and two other records not documented in Bahamas: Andros 1970 and in Eleuthera in 2004 (Purdy 2004 and Kirwan et al., 2019).

2 *Mareca penelope*/**Eurasian Wigeon**/Pato Lavanco Eurasiático: I modified the common name including the reference to the "Pato Lavanco": from "Pato Eurasiático" to "Pato Lavanco Eurasiático", due to its huge similarity with the species known in Cuba and in this way, it can be better associated locally.

3 *Streptopelia decaocto decaocto*/**Eurasian Collared-Dove (Eurasian)**/Tórtola de Collar: This is an invasive species that began to spread throughout Europe in the 1930s, later colonizing North America with an undetermined number of no more than 50 birds, which escaped from an aviary in Nassau (Bahamas) in 1974 (Smith 1987), were already breeding in 1975 and dispersed to adjacent territories such as Andros in 1978-1979 (Smith 1987). In the 80's it was observed breeding in the Florida Keys (Isla Morada) and between 1986 and 1996 there was a rapid population increase in North America, dispersing to Mexico and Caribbean islands, in the latter apparently via "jump" dispersal (Garrido and Kirkconnell 1990, Romagosa and Lavisky 2000, Romagosa and Mlodinow 2022). The first record of the species in Cuba was made in the city of Havana in 1990 (Garrido and Kirkconnell 1990). Despite this recent huge expansion, there are previous records in North America when Bailey (1922) makes the first report for Florida and then finds new pairs from Key Biscayne, Miami, Florida, from a successful introduction carried out in the 1930s, which increased to more than 300 individuals, later disappearing for unknown reasons (Bailey 1935). Smith (1987) refers to other feral populations of this species, prior to this last great expansion; such as those registered in 1929 in California (Smith 1987), which apparently persisted until the 1980s. Another population was recorded in 1953 in St. Petersburg, Florida (Grimes 1953), which also persisted until the late 1980s too. Reviewing the bird collection of the Joaquín de la Vara de Gibara Natural History Museum in Holguín, I found three specimens belonging to this species, two of them badly deteriorated so they did not present any color, perhaps because they belonged to the domestic variety (No. 0-320: December 16, 1951 and No. 0-321: January 20, 1952) and No. 0-342, which, despite its state of deterioration in terms of color, the diagnostic characters of this species can be perfectly appreciated (Historical Record , 1949), such as the dark band on the nape. This specimen was collected by Máximo Hernández on March 4, 1949. What is interesting about these records lies in the fact that they were made in rural areas and on dates as early as 1949, 1951 and 1952, and collected in the towns of Cupeicillo, Embarcadero and Los Hoyos respectively, all in the surroundings of Gibara, the earliest records for the Caribbean area. There are no references to the existence of established populations of this species in the area, so these could have been vagrant individuals arriving from exogenous populations, such as those mentioned in Florida, matching with this date range. Two of the specimens were collected only a few weeks apart from adjacent locations, which could suggest the existence of several individuals. The specimens involved (at least two of them 0-320 and 0-321) do not seem to belong to the wild variety, due to their white coloration, absence of gray lower coverts and pale primaries, which may also be related to deterioration caused by continuous exposure to light and poor storage conditions.

[4] *Zenaida macroura carolinensis*/**Mourning Dove**/Paloma Rabiche: In the previous issue it had been considered as a synonym of *Z. m. macroura* due to the significant overlap of characters and the poor existence of diagnostic characters that would allow them to be separated, however, and given that it has still been maintained on the lists by different authorities such as Clements et al. (2022) and Birds of The World (2022), I have decided include it again, however the separation of both forms in the field is extremely complicated and uncertain.

[5] *Chordeiles gundlachii vicinus*/**Antillean Nighthawk**/Querequeté: The absence of diagnostic characters of differentiation between the nominal race and *vicinus* is confusing and treated as invalid by some authors (Bond 1956 and Monroe 1965), the first one considering it as only a gray morph of *gundlachii*. More detailed studies on the taxonomic status of both populations, from Cuba and the Bahamas, are required due to weak differences in color and rusty tone distribution. Some authors have suggested for other close species of the genus a possible adaptation to the geographical conditions and a parallelism with the coloration of the soil of each site (Selander 1954, Eisenmann 1962), which is possible to observe between populations within Cuba, where various color morphs differ and show a marked interindividual variation, from typical dark patterns (Correa 2022) to more reddish (David Syzdek 2022) and lighter (Jovel 2022), also perceptible among juveniles (Jovel 2020). Kirkconnell et al. (2020) mention records of this form for different localities in the east and west of the island, however, the identification of these specimens remains pending, taking into account all the previous details and the range of variation of this form in Cuba.

[6] *Antrostomus cubanensis*/**Cuban Nightjar**/Guabairo: Recently validated by the 2022 eBird Taxonomic Update as a revision that begins the process of alignment of world checklists through the collaborative WGAC (Working Group Avian Checklists) (eBird 2022). This review only refers to the fact that they were separated based on subtle vocal differences, however they neglected to comment that in addition, there are morphological and color differences that allow easy differentiation of both populations. *A. ekmani* from Hispaniola is darker and has a slightly longer tail with the white band extending almost to the base of the tail, while in *A. cubanensis* this is limited to a small distal patch; the lower tail coverts in *A. ekmanii* are practically unbarred (Garrido and Reynard 1998) unlike that *A. cubanensis* where they are completely barred.

[7] *Nyctibius jamaicensis* ssp. (cf. *jamaicensis*)/**Northern Potoo (Caribbean)**/Potú: The explorations in search for this species have not yet found the bird in the wild, however it was possible to obtain the first photo of a live bird (RARC 2022d), captured by inmates in the surroundings of the juvenile prison of Santa Cruz, in the vicinity of Holguín. The inmates found a specimen and captured it while they were collecting wood to make charcoal. They took the bird to the farm areas of the detention center and placed it on a stump that they used to crush cassava for poultry. According to what Carlos Pupo (Karlos Ross) and I were told, the bird was there for at least two or three days and then disappeared. The vegetation conditions are perfectly propitious for the existence of this species, predominating the *Lysiloma* sp. or Soplillo trees as they are known locally, whose trunk is whitish in color. The forest in this area does not exceed an average height of 23 feet (7 mt) and grows on a loamy soil. The only existing photo was taken by a prison officer with a very low-resolution cell phone, which was recovered by Ross, however it is possible to observe the diagnostic characteristics that identify this species, but it denotes differences with respect to the populations known for Jamaica and Hispaniola. Together with Ross, we visited the place accompanied by "Raulito", a former prisoner who had witnessed the discovery. This information had previously been provided to us by Maikel Prieto Rivas, who had been the recipient of the first two specimens in the same area, he was also in the detention center serving a sentence and told us that during his stay there he had seen adult birds and chicks, for which he contacted us at that time, however the limitations generated by the COVID-19 pandemic restricted movement and prohibited contact with inmates for health security issues. The Holguín Birdwatching Club recently made visits to the area but it was not possible to obtain any records.

[8] *Cypseloides niger niger*/**Black Swift (niger)**/Vencejo Negro: During my stay for several months in the village of El Recreo, Baracoa, Guantánamo, I was able to continuously observe groups of Black Swifts (Navarro, 2022b) from the house of my friend Wisdenilde Navarro (alias El Indio

de Humboldt) in the valley located behind and adjacent to the internal coastal zone of Taco Bay. The observations involved courtship behaviors and they suddenly disappeared just at twilight along with Cave Swallows (*Petrochelidon fulva*), which led us to the assumption that the refuge was located nearby. Later we set about locating it and found that they were using a coastal cave known as Cueva de las Golondrinas, located on the edge of the coastal cliff inside Taco Bay, access to which is only possible by sea. Jeikel Navarro, son of "Indio" had access to said cave and was able to confirm that it was used as a refuge. Due to the inaccessibility of the site; it was not possible for him to verify the existence of nests. The observations were made in the second half of May, so it could be expected that they were nesting in this site, since the dates match with what was reported by Marín and Sánchez (1998). According to personal communication from the cited source, the birds entered the shadowy area of the cave where the rock was kept moist by percolating water from the surface of the limestone massif, which could not verify the existence of nests. In Cuba this swift has only been found nesting in the mountains of the central massif of Topes de Collantes (Montes-Espín and García-Rivera 2010). If this fact is verified, it would be the first record of nesting of the nominal subspecies in coastal areas, only the race *C. n. borealis* has been reported nesting in coastal areas (Gunn et al., 2022).

9 *Cyanolimnas cerverai*/**Zapata Rail**/Gallinuela de Santo Tomás: Brown et al. (2022) consider unjustified retaining the genus *Cyanolymnas* for Zapata Rail, for which they are based on morphological and phylogenetic characters. Despite the fact that said article provides a literally probable and necessary perspective, which suggests the potential roots of the Cuban species, I do not consider it appropriate to assume as valid *per se*, not recognizing the status of the genus. The article is interesting but simple and without sufficient comparative morphological analyzes to give absolute support to this result. On the other hand it is based on material from a single and ancient specimen. Delegitimizing the validity of a genus must be supported by an in-depth analysis and with more solid comparative arguments, assuming modifications on the interpretation of specific results only leads to making the taxonomic and nomenclatural panorama more complex with the already known back and forward paths. It is unfortunate that an effort like this did not consider extending sampling material from any of the other 13 specimens in collections.

10 *Recurvirostra americana*/**American Avocet**/Avoceta Americana: My colleague Omar Labrada recently informed me that he continues to find nests of this species in the wetlands of the Cienaga de Birama, which belongs to the Delta del Cauto Wildlife Refuge, Granma.

11 *Calidris fuscicollis*/**White-rumped Sandpiper**/Zarapico de Rabadilla Blanca: This species is quite common as a transient and it is possible to observe almost all year round, except in the months of December and January. There is a record in January by Arturo Kirkconnell in Cayo Coco (Kirkconnell et al., 2020), however additional information is needed to prove that it is not a fortuitous event.

12 *Phalaropus lobatus*/**Red-necked Phalarope**/Zarapico Nadador: Apparently the species in Cuba could be more frequent than estimated. In addition to the records mentioned by Kirkconnell et al., 2020, four new records were added between 2020 and the current year for different locations in Cuba, both in the east and in the west (González 2021, Verdecia 2021, Mantilla 2022, Navarro 2022c). Definitively, the specimen referred to this species belonging to the Joaquín de la Vara collection and mentioned by Bond (Kirkconnell et al., 2020) is not valid and constituted an identification error. In this collection only two specimens of this type of bird were registered, one of them 0-233 collected on December 10, 1963 in Gibara still in the Gibara Museum and the second registered as *Lobipes lobatus* (Ortega-Piferrer 1983). That It was sent to the former Cuban Academy of Sciences, currently in the IES collection (without data and with a handwritten text on the base that reads "OJO sin identificar"), Havana and which belongs to *Phalaropus fulicarius*. Therefore, the Gibara record should not be considered as valid.

13 *Stercorarius pomarinus*/**Pomarine Jaeger**/Estercorario Pomarino: Kirkconnell et al., 2020 mentioned a possible error in the collection data of one of the two specimens from the Joaquín de la Vara de Gibara collection (O-180), without explaining details. There really is an inconsistency between the date given by Bond in 1964 (April 21, 1960, Pueblo Nuevo) and the data that currently exists in the catalog records of the Gibara Natural History Museum (April 21,

1970, Bahía de Gibara). In any case, the location would be in the limits of Gibara and the date must be corrected to 1960, since this was mentioned by Bond in 1964.

[14] *Rissa tridactyla*/**Black-legged Kittiwake**/Gallego Patinegro: There is uncertainty regarding the Kirkconnell et al., 2020 reference to the existence of four specimens in the Joaquín de la Vara from Gibara collection. I have reviewed this collection on several occasions and I have not been able to find references for them. Said authors mention the specimen number 0-234 as captured on April 3, 1946, however, in the data of said museum's catalog it appears as collected in December 1963. Some specimens of this collection were donated to the former Academy of Sciences of Cuba; however, there is no reference that this species had been involved (Ortega-Piferrer 1983). Due to the above, I have the impression that it is an error to consider the existence of these four specimens, when the physical evidence indicates that only one exists, Kirkconnell et al. (2020) mention different dates, all from Gibara and belonging to the Joaquín de la Vara collection and in which they talk about the Bond record (1964). It is striking that this date (Dec. 1954) is repeated when talking about *Xema sabini*, so it could constitute a confusion, adding to it furthermore, Bond never reviewed this material, but rather received the information from Orlando Garrido, who examined and identified it and transferred the data to him. Therefore, there is no valid reason to consider the existence of four records in said collection, when, instead, it is valid to mention only one.

[15] *Xema sabini sabini*/**Sabine's Gull**/Gallego de Cola Ahorquillada: The third record for Cuba was made by Hernández 2023, January 5th 2023 in Playa El Chivo, Havana. Two former records from Gibara, Dec. 1954 (Bond 1964) and Guanahacabibes Peninsula, Oct. 28, 1999 (Llanes 2016).

[16] *Larus delawarensis*/**Ring-billed Gull**/Gallego Real: Kirkconnell et al., 2020 refer to the fact that the specimen referred to in Bond 1964 (pg. 11) from the Joaquín de la Vara de Gibara collection is lost. However, it is striking that the specimen 0-234 assigned to *Rissa tridactyla* coincidentally has a transverse black stripe on its beak in the manner of a Ring-billed Gull (*Larus delawarensis*) (Historical Records 1963) and is from 1963, as is the data provided by Bond, so the reference to a specimen from this collection assigned to *L. delawarensis* could have constituted an identification error, based on this diagnostic character and also aberrant for the Black-legged Kittiwake. This would be an assumption to take into consideration since there is no other material belonging to *L. delawarensis* in this collection and that Bond himself, according to his own comments, never physically saw. Taking into account the above, I question the validity of the record of *L. delawarensis* in the Joaquín de la Vara collection, until it is possible to clarify its location or real existence.

[17] *Sterna paradisaea*/**Arctic Tern**/Gaviota Ártica: Known so far on the basis of two specimens (Kirkconnell et al., 2020). There is a recent record, supported by photos, from south of Los Palacios in Pinar del Río (Rodolfo Castro pers. comm. 2022). Gundlach (1873) mentioned this species for Cuba and reported it having been observed only once in Batabanó. However, in the 1893 edition he apparently substituted the identification of the specimens (without explanation) and only mentioned the Roseate Gull (*Sterna dougallii*), commenting that it had only been observed on the southern coast of Cuba, which agrees with the record of his work from 1873. In the Ragues catalog (1914), he mentions that there are two specimens with the number 235 in the collection of Gundlach. Recently Carlos Hernández, curator of the IES collection, kindly sent me photos of said Gundlach specimens, currently in the IES collection and both: an adult and a juvenile, originally identified as *S. paradisaea*, actually belong to *S. dougallii*.

[18] *Butorides virescens virescens*/**Green Heron**/Aguaitacaimán: The *brunnescens* form was described as a species and later considered to have "color phase" status (Oberholser 1912), although it is actually a color morph and not a phase. Oberholser (1912) and Kirkconnell et al., (2020) erred in stating that it was described by Lembeye 1950 and by Gundlach and Cabanis in 1956 (really Gundlach, 1856) respectively. This should be corrected as it was actually described by Gundlach in Lembeye in 1950. In his book "Aves de la Isla de Cuba", Lembeye makes it explicit that the authorship is Gundlach's and not his. I have observed this morph with some frequency in different locations in Cuba; recently I had the opportunity to photograph one in the area of the Los Colorados Archipelago, Viñales, Pinar del Río (Navarro 2022c).

19 *Plegadis chihi*/**White-faced Ibis**/Coco Cariblanco: Maikel Cañizares observed three adult individuals that she identified as belonging to this species (Cañizares 2022), which showed the field marks of the complete white border around the face, however, it was not possible for him to obtain photos, so as an eBird reviewer I suggested moving to the Glossy/White-faced Ibis option. However, it should be taken into consideration that this species could be underestimated due to its great resemblance to the Old World species and that in Cuba it is common in wetlands. I consider it important to mention that Garrido, in a letter sent to James Bond on August 25, 1977, comments that Joaquín de la Vara had captured a specimen in Gibara that could potentially belong to this species: "La Vara though he had caught a *Plegadis chihi*, because the fresh bird has a ring of white around the face and even on the throat...", however he later comments that after being prepared, the bird gradually lost this white color and according to Garrido's own examination it seemed more like a Glossy Ibis (*P.facinellus*).

20 *Coragyps atratus atratus*/**Black Vulture**/Zopilote: Recently my colleague Yaroddys Rodriguez and I, with the support of Odanel Almeida†, visited the town of Itabo, Martí in Matanzas and we were able to verify the existence of a population of at least 50 individuals (Navarro 2022d). These were observed in the Itabo dam and flying over a wide area that covered up to the coast. Apparently there is also a population nucleus within the Ciénaga de Zapata, where it has been frequently observed and photographed (eBird 2022c).

21 *Chondrohierax wilsonii*/**Cuban Kite**/Gavilán Caguarero: Long considered conspecific with *Ch. uncinatus*, a detailed historical compilation and analysis was discussed by Kirwan et al., 2022. Re-evaluated and validated at a specific level and returned to its original status in AOS Supplement 63 (Chesser et al., 2022), based on pronounced differences in color, morphometry, variation, and molecular studies.

22 *Accipiter striatus fringilloides*/**Sharp-shinned Hawk**/Gavilancito: Originally described by Vigors as a species (Vigors 1828). Although some authors suggest that the article was described in 1827, this volume actually includes publications between January 1827 and April 1828 and places the latter as the date of publication. This form is then treated together with other relative taxa as conspecific with *A. striatus* (Hellmayr and Conover 1949, Friedman 1950, AOU 1998). There is extensive inter and intrapopulation variation in the forms considered within *striatus*, however many of them may well categorize for species status. In the previous issue (Navarro 2022a) I commented on the recent results of molecular studies (Catanach 2020), which place it as genetically different from the rest of the Caribbean (*striatus* and *venator*) and continental (*velox*) forms. The results of our recent studies with the population of the eastern region of Cuba reinforce the criterion of their specific separation, allowing us to collect important information that shows significant differences in vocalizations, reproduction and coloration with respect to the rest of the populations. In my opinion, the *fringilloides* form is completely different and should be treated as a valid species. If approved, I propose to name it Gavilancito Cubano, which is the translation of Cuban Sharp-shinned Hawk, a name adopted by Hellmayr and Conover in 1949 to refer to the Cuban population.

23 *Accipiter gundlachi*/**Gundlach's Hawk**/Gavilán Colilargo: An unusual record of a bird with similar characteristics to a male Gundlach's Hawk was photographed in Cape Coral on January 1, 2023 at 9:36 AM (www.reddit.com/user/ZoZoBettaLover1305/), perching on the roof of a house. The bird had the typical pattern of *A. gundlachi* males, flat gray chest and reddish-brown barred lower abdomen, reddish-brown tights with fine white bars. It would not be unusual for a bird like this to arrive on the Florida coast, as has happened with other smaller and sedentary birds, if verified, this would be the first record of this species for North America. The possibility that it was an aberrant pattern of *A. cooperii* should not be ruled out.

24 *Accipiter gundlachi wileyi*/**Gundlach's Hawk**/Gavilán Colilargo: On the validity of the subspecies *A. g. wileyi*, I consider this form should be treated with caution and more complete taxonomic studies needs to carried out before being validated as such. I carried out a detailed analysis of the original description in Wotskow (1991), based on my current experiences with different populations throughout Cuba (Guantánamo, Holguín, Ciego de Ávila, Havana and Pinar del Río provinces), in which I had the opportunity to study and photograph several couples simultaneously and with the help of many colleagues. Regardless of the fact that the eastern

populations of this species could show geographical variations in their color pattern, it was not possible to validate the following diagnostic characters provided by its author, as there is a wide margin of overlap in these characters, therefore the subspecies is not diagnosable. Firstly, the author did not consider, or at least does not appear in the description, the wide interindividual and intrapopulation variation of the species throughout the archipelago, nor the sexual dimorphism present, where males not only show differences in size, but also in the color pattern. They have a flat gray chest and the design of reddish bands is limited to the underbelly, being able to extend more or less, being a variable character. The females, on the other hand, have this pattern of bars extended to the chest and throat which overlap with the gray area of the chest, giving it a dirty appearance and less barred towards the chest. The density of the reddish bars is variable, from birds with broader white bars and others almost entirely rusty ventrally, with only white dots.

[25] *Buteo swainsoni*/**Swainson's Hawk**/Gavilán de Swainson: At the beginning of August 2022 I was able to photograph an individual flying at a considerable height near the town of Los Hoyos, Viñales, Pinar del Río (Navarro, 2022e), this constitutes the fifth documented record for Cuba. Taking into account the wide geographical distribution of the observations, it is very likely that this species is more frequent and is being underestimated because it seems to pass as a passage migrant at a considerable height, often out of sight of observers and in other cases confused with some other species of local *Buteo*.

[26] *Athene cunicularia*/**Burrowing Owl**/Sijú de Sabana: Barbour 1943 and Kirkconnell et al., 2020 erroneously refer that the first record of the species was the material collected by Gaston Villalba in Campo Florido, Havana. Bond refers to a record of the species for Cuba (Bond 1943), and mentions it as accidental in his 1936 edition (Bond 1936), without commenting on its origin or details, later the author himself mentions the Ramsden specimen (Bond 1950 and Bond 1956). Garrido (2001) refers to these Bond publications and mentions the Ramsden specimen, without specifying details. Apparently, in the first mentions, its authors were unaware that the first specimen of this species and the first record for Cuba was made by Charles T. Ramsden in 1915. During a visit I made in October 2022 with my colleague Yaroddys Rodríguez to the Charles Ramsden Museum of the Universidad de Oriente in Santiago de Cuba, we were able to examine this specimen and its accessory documentation (History Records, 1915). The specimen was collected by Ramsdem himself on March 20, 1915 in San Carlos, Guantanamo, in a secondarily forested area of about three acres (1.2 km2) surrounded by sugar cane plantations and pastures, all of the above referred to by Ramsden in an original letter to Bond dated 15 September 1942, examined by me. There is an article published in "La Independencia", Santiago de Cuba´s local newspaper of May 12, 1915 and preserved in the museum (Historical Records, 1915). The specimen was sent to J. H. Riley who showed it to Robert Ridgway for identification. The bird was identified as belonging to the *floridana* form (*Speotyto floridana dominicensis*= *S. cunicularia floridana*) (Bond 1956), a population that Garrido (2001) later described as a different subspecies (*A. c. guantanamensis*), and it is interesting that he did not mention or include this material within the type series or commented on the description.

[27] *Dryocopus pileatus*/**Pileated Woodpeaker**/Carpintero Norteamericano: First record for Cuba, for more details see **1.18 New Records and Other Additions**, p. 19.

[28] *Caracara plancus cheriway*/**Crested Caracara**/Caraira: The subspecies *C. c. auduboni*, usually referred to Florida populations based on light morphometric and color characters. Subsequently Dove and Banks (1999) consider this subspecies, along with others, synonymous with *cheriway*, which is currently followed by most ornithological authorities in the area (Clements et al., 2022, Morrison and Dwyer 2021).

[29] *Tyrannus savana*/**Fork-tailed Flycatcher**/Pitirre de Cola Ahorquillada: Bond 1936 reports it as accidental in Cuba based on the Ramsden record and later mentions it based on two records (Bond 1956), the most recent being the one referring to this species from Los Sitios, Ensenada de Guadiana and collected on November 11, 1952 by R. Delgado (Kirkconnell 2020). There is another record without any other data referring to the month of February (Garrido and Kirkconnell 2000), these last authors apparently were unaware of the existence of the Ramsden record from 1931 or made an erroneous reference. According to a letter sent to James Bond,

Ramsden himself comments on the detailed description of the bird, which was captured on January 18, 1931 in the Vista Alegre neighborhood, Santiago de Cuba, where it spent several days flying and feeding along with other Tyrannids, as explained by Ramsden himself in said letter, reviewed by me. I consider it important to comment on the validity of the other two record mentions for Cuba, the only one apparently confirmed must be that of Ramsden. The February record in Garrido and Kirkconnell (2000) and Kirkconnell et al. (2020) does not have confirmed evidence and the one by R. Delgado in November 1952 is confusing since according to these authors the specimen is lost and the specimen is not mentioned with a catalog number. However, there is a specimen of *T. forficatus* (MFP 13.000976) in the same collection with almost identical collection data, whose difference lies only in the day, which in my opinion generates uncertainty regarding the validity of the same. There is a record of La Lisa, Havana (Luis del Castillo 2022), of which it was not possible to obtain photos, however the colleague Sergio Luis del Castillo immediately contacted me and was able to provide me with sufficient details to be valid, however I suggested that it be settled in eBird as *Tyrannus* sp.

30 *Empidonax traillii*/**Willow Flycatcher**/Bobito de los Sauces: In the previous edition (Navarro 2022a) I referred to keeping the name used in previous references, however I have considered that this name should not be used for this species, since it is the denomination for those individuals or specimens that cannot be identified as *E. alnorum* or *E. traillii*, following Pyle 1997 (Navarro 2019), since they have overlapping characters. Therefore, I propose to assign the local name in Cuba as "Bobito de los Sauces", taking into account the homologation with the names in English and Spanish (SEO), to which the name "Mosquero" was replaced by the local "Bobito".

31 *Lanius* sp. prob. *L. ludovicianus*/**Shrike sp. (probably Loggerhead Shrike)**/Alcaudón (prob. Americano): First record for Cuba, see comments at **1.18 New Records and Other Additions**, p. 20.

32 *Stelgidopteryx serripennis*/**Northern Rough-winged Swallow**/Golondrina de Alas Ásperas: The reference to the subspecies *S. s. psammochroa* in Kirkconnell et al., 2020 should be treated with caution, since these authors did not examine the specimen and the differences between the two subspecies are so subtle that many consider the species monotypic and whose differences are associated with clinal variations (De Jong 2020).

33 *Progne dominicensis*/**Caribbean Martin**/Golondrina Caribeña: The first record of this species was made by Navarro 2019 in northern Holguín. Ricel Polán recently observed several individuals in the south of the province of Granma, in the east of the island, and made the first nesting record of the species in Cuba (Polán 2022a). On April 23 a couple was observed carrying fibers with which they built the nest in a hole inside a public lighting lamp, where both parents were observed feeding the chicks on June 1 (Polán 2022b). The arrival of this small population in southern eastern Cuba may be related to the expansion of the population from Jamaica, which during spring migration could reach neighboring territories, usually outside the range of distribution. It would be important to monitor the populations of *Progne* swallows in eastern Cuba, especially on the southern coast and the eastern extreme (Maisí), since it might not be an isolated phenomenon. The photo of a female *Progne*, assigned to Cuban Martin, was taken in areas of the Guantánamo Naval Base (Fidler 2018) and could belong to this species, since in addition to being an early record, it shows a high contrast in the lower parts and very white belly. Caribbean Martin has been reported for Cuba in a date range between April and August (eBird 2022c).

34 *Bombycilla garrulus* (prob. *pallidiceps*)/**Bohemian Waxwing**/Picotero Europeo: This species was moved to the main list from the unconfirmed list, since it had been mentioned by Garrido and González (1980) based on Laudelino Bueno's comment, without validating details. This is the first record for Cuba and the Antilles, which has been confirmed by examining the illustration made by Laudelino Bueno in his diaries, these have been carefully preserved by his daughter Alicia Bueno, who kindly allowed us to review them and obtain photos. Apparently Laudelino had two records, however in the illustration that appeared in one of his diaries, he only comments on one of them when he says "traje el Picotero". Garrido makes an extended comment in a letter sent to James Bond, dated July 19, 1978 kindly sent by Garrido to be scanned and carefully examined by me. More details in **1.18 New Records and Other Additions**, p. 20.

[35] *Troglodytes aedon aedon*/**House Wren (Northern)**/Troglodita Americano: Change linear sequence following Chesser et al., 2022.

[36] *Ferminia cerverai*/**Zapata Wren**/Ferminia: Troglodita Americano: Change linear sequence following Chesser et al., 2022.

[37] *Mimus gundlachii*/**Bahama Mockingbird**/Sinsonte Prieto: On a recent visit to the Charles Ramsden collection of the Universidad de Oriente in October 2022, a specimen (without data) caught my attention in the display area in showcases, which was identified as Brown Thrasher (*Toxostoma rufum*). Upon examination, I identified it as belonging to the Bahama Mockingbird. Correspondence dated December 28, 1912 sent to Ramsden by W. E. C. Todd of the Carneige Museum explains the details of this specimen; it was donated to Ramsden and comes from Great Inagua.

[38] *Oenanthe oenanthe* prob. *leucorhoa*/**Northern Wheatear (Greenland)**/Tordo del Ártico: Separated by decision of The Working Group Avian Checklists (WGAC) in eBird 2022 Taxonomy Update, based on differences in plumage color pattern and area of distribution. As a result, Northern Wheatear (*Oenanthe oenanthe*) and Atlas Wheatear (*Oenanthe seebohmi*) from North Africa are now recognized as separate species.

[39] *Spinus tristis* sp. (prob. *tristis*)/**American Goldfinch**/Jilguero Americano: I consider it appropriate to modify the common name of this species, taking into account that it is very rare in Cuba and even the use of a local name is not widespread, as well as on the basis that the name of Yellow Sparrow (Navarro 2022) was not suitable, since it is probably not a Sparrow, but closer to the Goldfinch, therefore I propose to call it American Goldfinch, adapting the standardized name according to SEO (Yankee Goldfinch), whose designation in the latter alludes to a pejorative term in the Spanish spoken in Cuba, and for which the term "American" is used to designate that which comes from North America in local slang.

[40] *Calcarius lapponicus lapponicus*/**Lapland Longspur**/Escribano Lapón: Two registries had been previously validated for Cuba (Navarro 2019 and Navarro 2020). The third record was made on October 1, 2022 in the town of Las Ovas, Pinar del Río, after the passage of the destructive Hurricane Ian (September 29, 2022). It was captured in a trap cage by a local "bird trapper" (RARC 2022b).

[41] *Junco hyemalis hyemalis*/**Dark-eyed Junco**/Junco de Ojos Oscuros: Only four records of this species were known for Cuba, two without graphic documentation and two with photographs, the latter captured by local "bird trappers" (Navarro 2022). A new individual was a female of the nominal form, captured on October 22 by a "bird trapper" in the town of Pálpite, Ciénaga de Zapata (RARC 2022c), constituting the third documented record of the species for the archipelago.

[42] *Melospiza melodia*/**Song Sparrow**/Gorrión Cantor: First record for Cuba, see details in **1.18 New Records and Other Additions**, p. 20.

[43] *Spindalis zena*/**Western Spindalis**/Cabrero: It is very interesting that after the passage of the destructive Hurricane Ian through Cuba, on September 29, 2022, numerous records of Western Spindalis began to be reported in areas where they were not usual before, even in numerically unusual flocks, this was reported by local birdwatchers and "bird trappers" in Havana. Coincidentally, the second record of the Cuban subspecies for Florida also occurred in this period (Groskopf, John 2022, Gles, L. 2022), which demonstrates the influence of hurricanes on the distribution of bird species. A similar situation occured around these same dates with small groups of Red-legged Honeycreepers that apparently came from Cuba and were transported by this powerful category 3 and 4 hurricane.

[44] *Xanthocephalus xanthocephalus*/**Yellow-headed Blackbird**/Mayito de Cabeza Amarilla: A very rare species for Cuba and the rest of the Antilles, known from only five records in Cuba (Kirkconnell et al., 2020). I found a very diagnostic illustration, probably a female (Historical Records 1978), with its respective description: "Bird bigger than a Totí... it is black, with a yellow throat", in one of Laudelino Bueno's diaries, a specimen captured on 1 November 1978 in La

Papelera, Cárdenas, Matanzas and donated to him by an unspecified person. This constitutes the sixth record for Cuba.

45 *Icterus spurius*/**Orchard Oriole (Orchard)**/Turpial de Huertos: Kirkconnell et al., 2020 suggest the possibility that it will eventually be a winter resident, which is also likely according to the data provided by eBird (eBird 2022c).

46 *Molothrus ater ater*/**Brown-headed Cowbird**/Pajaro Vaquero Americano: Only known from two specimens (Kirkconnell et al., 2020). To these two are added three recent records: from May 15, 2020 in Cayo Juan García, Pinar del Río (Beltrán-Casanueva 2020), January and February 2022 in Vedado and Cerro, Havana (Cañizares-Morera 2022, Vega 2022) and April 2022 north of Ciego de Ávila (Rodríguez-Castañeda 2022), with which there would be a total of five records for Cuba. It is highly probable that the species is more frequent in Cuba than is estimated; therefore, I have decided to modify the category of abundance from Very Rare to Rare.

47 *Quiscalus mexicanus*/**Great-tailed Grackle**/Chichinguaco Mexicano: First record for Cuba, for more details see **1.18 New Records and Other Additions**, p. 20.

48 *Oporornis agilis*/**Connecticut Warbler**/Bijirita de Connecticut: Several reports have been made of this species, however not all of them have been satisfactorily validated (Kirkconnell et al., 2020). The first record with validation potential was that of Plasencia et al. (2019), although I had the opportunity to see a photo, unfortunately these data have not been made public on any platform that allows referencing it, the article does not incorporate photos nor provide enough details to be validated (see **1.19. About the new records and reports of rare birds**, p. 20). Only two new records have been documented through photos: Cayo Santa María, October 26, 2019 (Arias 2019, Ruiz et al., in press) and a second record made on board a cruise ship near the Cuban coast on October 15, 2022 (Carpenter 2022).

49 *Setophaga petechia rubiginosa*/**Yellow Warbler**/Canario de Manglar: From the review of the material in the IES collection and the examination of the correspondence between Orlando Garrido and James Bond (in a letter of March 31, 1969), the latter refers to the impossibility of separating this subspecies based on the material that Garrido had collected, therefore I have decided to remove this shape from the main list.

50 *Setophaga coronata*/**Yellow-rumped Warbler**/Bijirita Coronada: The second sighting of the species for Cuba was recorded by photos in Guanahacabibes (Lopez-del Castillo et al., in press).

51 *Setophaga townsendi*/**Townsend's Warbler**/Bijirita de Townsend: Kirkconnell et al., 2020 mention only one confirmed record of this species for Cuba, however they apparently were unaware of a photographic record (four photos) on the www.Observation.org site, which was made by Garry Bakker on the trail to La Turba, Ciénaga de Zapata, Matanzas, on April 1, 2017 (Bakker 2017), which makes it the second record of this species for Cuba.

52 *Piranga ludoviciana*/**Western Tanager**/Cardenal del Oeste: There is an unconfirmed visual record of Leonardo Milan, who is a local ranger in Ciénaga de Zapata. This record (Milan 2022) was not validated due to the absence of graphic evidence; however, I was able to talk by phone with the observer, who provided me with detailed evidence of it.

53 *Pheucticus melanocephalus*/**Black-headed Grosbeak**/Degollado Cabecinegro: I modified the common name from "Picogrueso Cabecinegro" to "Degollado Cabecinegro", being a very rare species in Cuba it is not known by any common name, so I adjusted the name given to "Degollado", a very similar species to associate it with another species that is well known on the island. The "bird trappers" in Cuba use this name (Degollado) to associate it with similar species.

54 *Volatinia jacarina splendens*/**Blue-black Grassquit**/Arrocero Negrito: Navarro, 2019 mentioned the probable cause of its arrival and refered to the ocurrence of huracán Alma. It is necessary to point out that Garrido and García-Montaña (1967) mentioned the occurrence weeks before the powerful hurricane Beulah. This type of high intensity hurricane has impacts on the movement of different species, see comments below on Red-legged Honeycrepper.

55 *Cyanerpes cyaneus carneipes*/**Red-legged Honeycreeper**/Aparecido de San Diego: Garrido (2001) considered the species as probably introduced, based on analysis of László Passuth's historical novel, "El Diós de la Lluvia Llora sobre México" (originally published in 1938 in an

edition translated into Spanish in 1975), in which it is not possible to find explicit reference to this fact, on the other hand, the work of this author does not constitute a historical document. Passuth recreated the history of the discovery in works of fiction and although he carried out a detailed study of the historical processes, it should not be used as a reference. Therefore, I consider that there is no reason to keep this species as introduced. The origin of the Cuban population may be related to meteorological dispersal processes in the recent past, which is why it may not have differentiated from Central American populations. After Hurricane Ian, at the end of September 2022, there were dissimilar sightings in Florida and the southwestern coast of the continent, which involved more than one individual and most likely were different cases (eBird 2022d), which reinforces the theory of dispersion by meteorological events.

[56] *Streptopelia roseogrisea*/**African Collared-Dove**/ Tórtola de Collar Africana: First record for Cuba see **1.18 New Records and Other Additions**, p. 20.

[57] *Pachyramphus polychopterus spp.*/**White-winged Becard**/Mosquero Cabezón de Alas Blancas: First record for Cuba and the Antilles, probably "ship assisted". See more data in **1.18 New Records and Other Additions**, p. 19.

[58] *Sylvia atricapilla*/**Eurasian Blackcap**/Curruca Capirotada (SEO): This species had been reported by Navarro and Fernández-Ordoñez (2017) and subsequently totally removed from the lists, along with others that had suspiciously been previously recorded for Cuba, based on the fact that it was not possible to determine at that time the origin of the species (Navarro 2019). In mid-2022 and thanks to the help of my colleague Yaroddys Rodríguez, it was possible to contact by video call Pavel González (local bird trapper from Santa Fé, Havana), the person who had captured these birds, who currently resides in Europe. He alleges that he could only give credit to two of the species: Eurasian Blackcap (*S. atricapilla*) and Yellow-mantle Widowbird (*E. macroura*). According to this source, they were the only ones that had been captured by him and not the rest of the species, which apparently had been obtained by exchange and whose information is quite uncertain. He alleges that he captured *S. atricapilla* along with a flock of other warbler species using a mist net, during the fall migration in October 2012. Considering the possible veracity of this information, without giving absolute credence to what was expressed by him, I considered restoring this species to the lists and placing it on the list of exotics, introduced and of uncertain origin (Table 3).

[59] *Euplectes cf. hordaceus/afer*/**Bishop sp.**/Obispo sp.: Navarro (2019) corrected the original identification of the specimen and did not consider it within the main list (Navarro 2021). I should point out that the approach in Kirkconnell et al. (2020) on the identification of the species is incorrect; the great similarity between the females of *hordaceus* and *afer* did not allow me to make an accurate identification, which is why I decided to assume both taxa as probable, given an ambiguous identification. Kirkonnell et al., 2020 refer to it as *E. afer* without details of the diagnosis in each case, based on my previous criteria, but they did not take into account the ambiguity in the identification.

[60] *Euplectes macroura macroura*/**Yellow-mantled Widowbird**/Obispo Dorsiamarillo: Included in the supplementary list (Table 3), situation similar to the previous case of Eurasian Blackcap.

[61] *Haemorhous mexicanus* (prob. *frontalis*)/**House Finch**/Gorrión Mexicano: This species was moved to the list of exotic and introduced species based on my comments in Navarro 2022.

[62] *Chlorophanes spiza*/Green Honeycreeper/Mielerito Verde: Cory (1886) includes a record of *Chlorophanes atricapilla= Ch. spiza* according to the specimen in his cabinet obtained by Sclater and Salvin labeled as coming from Cuba, probably escaped from captivity (Cory 1886).

[63] *Ploceus cucullatus*/**Village Weaver**/Tejedor Común: A record claimed without any comments or documentation was considered by Kirkconnell et al., 2005 and later invalidated by Navarro 2019 for lack of evidence. It is important to comment that apparently O. H. Garrido had sent a specimen or a description to James Bond for identification and in a letter dated March 3, 1965, James Bond confirmed the identification, explaining that it was undoubtedly a specimen escaped from captivity: "Your plocid would appear to be *Ploceus cucullatus* as you suggested. It is doubtless an escaped cage-bird. Garrido currently does not recall associated information or the origin of the record (Garrido pers. com. 2022).

64 *Icterus gularis*/**Altamira Oriole**/Turpial de Altamira: this species was reported from existing material in the Joaquín de la Vara de Gibara collection (Navarro and Reyes 2017). Taking into account that we have detected errors in the handling of the information associated with this collection, as well as the insufficiency of more coherent data in the archives and catalogues, I have preferred to move it to the list of unconfirmed until there is more reliable information, since it is a Central American and sedentary species.

65 *Passerina rositae*/**Rose-bellied Bunting**/Mariposa de Vientre Rosado: Mentioned in exchange of letters between James Bond and Orlando Garrido, March 21, 1967 (examined by me), probably confused with some hybrid or color form of the Painted Bunting (*P. ciris*), which share a similar pattern of coloration on the belly. Very unlikely any record of this species in Cuba because it is a very local endemism in Mexico, however the possibility of some imported specimen and escaped from captivity is not ruled out.

66 *Tigrisoma mexicanum*/**Bare-throated Tiger Heron**/Garza Tigre Mexicana: Suárez (2022) mentions this species under the common name of "Garza Tigre Mejicana", however, although it is accepted, the Royal Academy of the Spanish Language recommends the use of x for the word Mexico and all its meanings and does not recommend the use of the j in these cases. Therefore, I have modified this name in the list as "Garza Tigre Mexicana".

1.55. List of additions and modifications at species and subspecies level in the main list subsequent to previous issues of the Checklist

No. 1 (2017)

1. **Common Merganser** (*Mergus merganser*)
2. **Surf Scoter** (*Melanitta perspicillata*)
3. **Eurasian Wigeon** (*Mareca penelope*)
4. **Bahama Woodstar** (*Nesophlox evelynae*)
5. **Great Shearwater** (*Ardenna gravis*)
6. **Franklin's Gull** (*Leucophaeus pipixcan*)
7. **Ruff** (*Calidris pugnax*)
8. **Lesser Black-backed Gull** (*Larus fuscus*)
9. **Cooper's Hawk** (*Accipiter cooperii*)
10. **Mississippi Kite** (*Ictinia mississippiensis*)
11. **Swainson's Hawk** (*Buteo swainsoni*)
12. **Short-tailed Hawk** (*Buteo brachyurus*)
13. **Common Kingfisher** (*Alcedo atthis*)
14. **Red-and-green Macaw** (*Ara chloropterus*)
15. **Blue-and-yellow Macaw** (*Ara ararauna*)
16. **Scarlet Macaw** (*Ara macao*)
17. **Cassin's Kingbird** (*Tyrannus vociferans*)
18. **Vermilion Flycatcher** (*Pyrocephalus rubinus*)
19. **House Crow** (*Corvus splendens*)
20. **Hermit Thrush** (*Catharus guttatus*)
21. **Eurasian Blackcap** (*Sylvia atricapilla*); REMOVED
22. **American Pipit** (*Anthus rubescens*)
23. **Lapland Longspur** (*Calcarius lapponicus*)
24. **Dark-eyed Junco** (*Junco hyemalis* ssp.)
25. **Altamira Oriole** (*Icterus gularis*)
26. **Yellow-tailed Oriole** (*Icterus mesomelas*)
27. **Kirtland´s Warbler** (*Setophaga kirtlandii*)
28. **Black-throated Gray Warbler** (*Setophaga nigrescens*)
29. **Townsend's Warbler** (*Setophaga townsendi*)
30. **Blue-black Grassquit** (*Volatinia jacarina*)
31. **Rose-ringed Parakeet** (*Psittacula krameri*)
32. **White-eared Bubul** (*Pycnonotus leucotis*); REMOVED
33. **Red-faced Liocichla** (*Liocichla phoenicea*); REMOVED
34. **Red-billed Leiothrix** (*Leiothrix lutea*); REMOVED
35. **Crested Myna** (*Acridotheres cristatellus*); REMOVED
36. **White-winged Snowfinch** (*Montifringilla nivalis*); REMOVED
37. **Orange Bishop** (*Euplectes franciscanus*), ID amended prob. *hordaceus*
38. **Yellow-mantled Widowbird** (*Euplectes macroura*); REMOVED

No. 2 (2018-2019)

39. **King Rail (Northern)** (*Rallus elegans elegans*)
40. **Curlew Sandpiper** (*Calidris ferruginea*)
41. **Caribbean Martin** (*Progne dominicensis*)
42. **Chestnut Munia** (*Lonchura atricapilla*)
43. **Palm Warbler (Yellow)** (*Setophaga palmarum **hypochrysea***)
44. **Yellow-rumped Warbler (Audubon's)** (*Setophaga coronata **auduboni***)
45. **Wilson's Warbler (pileolata)** (*Cardellina pusilla **pileolata***)

No. 3 (2020)

46. **White-faced Ibis** (*Plegadis chihi*)
47. **Common Myna** (*Acridotheres tristis tristis*)
48. **House Finch** (*Haemorhous mexicanus*)
49. **Connecticut Warbler** (*Oporornis agilis*)

No. 4 (2021)

50. **Dark-eyed Junco (Pink-sided)** (*Junco hyemalis **mearnsi***)

No. 5 (2022)

51. **White-throated Sparrow**- white stripe form- (*Zonotrichia albicollis*)
52. **Great Blue Heron (Blue form, Ward´s Heron)** (*Ardea herodias **wardi***)
53. **Turkey Vulture (Northern)** (*Cathartes aura **septentrionalis***)

No. 6 (2023)

54. **Brant** (*Branta bernicla nigricans*)
55. **African Collared Dove** (*Streptopelia roseogrisea*)
56. **Pileated Woodpeaker** (*Dryocopus pileatus*)
57. **White-winged Becard** (*Pachyramphus polychopterus*)
58. **Shrike** sp. prob. **Loggerhead** (*Lanius* sp. prob. *ludovicianus*)
59. **Bohemian Waxwing** (*Bombicilla garrulus*)
60. **Song Sparrow** (*Melospiza melodia*)
61. **Great-tailed Grackle** (*Quiscalus mexicanus*)

1.56. Table 6: Cuban Birds, Numbers and Percentages

West Indian data follows Gerbracht and Levesque (draft), recent records were added

Categories	Total Numbers	%	vs
Taxonomy			
• Orders	26	100%	total
• Families	71	100%	total
• Genus	225	100%	total
• Species (main list)	402	100%	total
○ Cuban species in relation to the West Indies (WI)	708 (WI)	57%	vs total West Indies species (including recent extinctions)
Threatened			
• Species at risk of extinction + others with local assessment following González et al., 2012	47+9	14%	vs total Cuban species
• Threatened species, VU, EN and CR (following IUCN, 2015)	21	5%	vs total Cuban species
• Extinct (in recent times)	2	0.5%	vs total Cuban species
Endemism			
• Endemic Family	1	1.4%	vs total of Cuban families
• Endemic Genus	9	4%	vs total of Cuban genus
• Cuban Endemics (including extinct Cuban Macaw)	27+1†=28	7%	vs total Cuban species
• Endemic Subspecies	29	100%	total
• Other West Indian Endemics	20	5%	vs total Cuban species
○ Near Endemics	9	45%	vs other West Indian Endemics
• Cuban Endemics in relation to the West Indies	172 (WI)	16%	vs total West Indies Endemics
Abundance, Breeding and Resident			
• Common and Fairly Common	189	47%	vs total Cuban species
• Breeding Species	147	37%	vs total Cuban species
• Year Round (YR), (Partial Migrants included)*	153	38%	vs total Cuban species
• Partial Migrants (PM)	46	11%	vs total Cuban species
• Winter Residents (WR), including PM^{WR}	116	29%	vs total Cuban species
• Summer Residents (SR), including PM^{SR}	12	3%	vs total Cuban species
• Transients (T), (exclusive)	36	9%	vs total Cuban species
• Vagrants (V), (exclusive)	79	20%	vs total Cuban species
• Total Migratory Component*	289	72%	WR+SR+T+V+PM/Total number of Cuban birds

Categories	Total Numbers	%	vs
Distribution			
• Pan Cuban (PC)	160	*40%*	*vs* total Cuban species
• Quasi Cuban (QC)	36	*9%*	*vs* total Cuban species
• Regional (Rg)	4	*1%*	*vs* total Cuban species
• Open Water habitant (OW)	17	*4%*	*vs* total Cuban species
Introduced			
• Introduced Species (established species)	13	*3%*	*vs* total Cuban species
• Exotic species not established, introduced, probably escaped from captivity or vagrants from introduced populations (not considered part of the Cuban avifauna)	36	-	-
Unconfirmed forms (species and subspecies)	18 sp. +2ssp.	-	-

*Cuban birds cannot be placed in a "black and white" context when we speak about a Migrant or a Year Round component. There are forms (species and subspecies) showing both conditions. Some of them, like Ruddy Turnstone (*Arenaria interpres morinella*) formerly considered a Winter Resident in Cuba, remain Year Round in small numbers, while others like Sharp-shinned Hawk (*Accipiter striatus*) have a local Year Round population (*A. s. fringilloides*) and another migratory population (*A. s. velox*). That is why I decided to consider a category as "Migratory Component", hoping to achieve a better understanding of these phenomena. Partial Migrants (formerly considered in a Cuban local ornithological context as "Bimodal Residents", see p. 16) are those that are part migratory and part Year Round; consequently they should be counted twice to calculate each component. In any case, the conditions are perhaps more difficult to understand than expected.

1.57. References

American Ornithologists' Union (1998). *Check-list of North American Birds*. Seventh edition. American Ornithologists' Union, Washington, DC, USA.

Arias, A. (2019). eBird Checklist: https://ebird.org/checklist/S122660675. eBird: An online database of bird distribution and abundance [web application]. eBird, Ithaca, New York. Available: http://www.ebird.org. (Accessed: January 10, 2023).

Bailey, H. H. 1922. New addition to A.O.U Check-list of North American Birds. Oologist 39: 91.

Bailey, H. H. (1935). A new race of Ringed Turtle Dove (*Streptopelia risoria*) in the United States. Bailey Museum of Natural History Bulletin 9:1-2.

Bakker, G. 2017. Observation.org dataset, *Setophaga townsendi*. Acessed 31 de diciembre, 2022. Observation International y socios locales. https://observation.org/observation/136237004/

Barbour, T. (1943). *Cuban Ornithology, Memoirs of the Nuttall Ornithological Club*, Cambridge, Massachusetts, IX.

Beltran-Casanueva, R. (2020). eBird Checklist: https://ebird.org/checklist/S124987946. eBird: An online database of bird distribution and abundance [web application]. eBird, Ithaca, New York. Available: http://www.ebird.org. (Accessed: January 10, 2023).

Berthold, P. (2001). *Bird migration: a general survey. Second edition*. Oxford University Press, New York.

Billerman, S.M., B. K. Keeney, P. G. Rodewald, and T. S. Schulenberg (Editors) (2022). *Birds of the World*. Cornell Laboratory of Ornithology, Ithaca, NY, USA. https://birdsoftheworld.org/bow/home

Bond, J. (1936). *Birds of the West Indies*. Academy of Natural Sciences, Philadelphia.

Bond, J. (1943). Florida Burrowing Owl in Cuba. *Auk* 60: 105.

Bond, J. (1950). *Check-list of birds of the West Indies*. The Academy of Natural Sciences of Philadelphia; Third Edition.

Bond, J. (1956). *Check-list of birds of the West Indies*. Academy of Natural Sciences, Philadelphia. Fourth edition.

Bond, J. (1964). Ninth supplement to the *Check-list of birds of the West Indies* (1956). Academy of Natural Sciences, Philadelphia.

Bond, J. 1956. Check-list of birds of the West-Indies. Fourth edition. Academy of Natural Sciences, Philadelphia, 214 pp.

Brown A. F., Y. Lawrie, T. J. Shannon, J. M. Collinson, G. M. Kirwan, A. Kirkconnell & M. Stervander, 2022. First genetic data for the critically endangered Cuban endemic Zapata Rail *Cyanolimnas cerverai*, and the taxonomic implications. *Journal of Ornithology*, vol. 163, pp. 945–952.

Cañizares-Morera, M. (2022a). eBird Checklist: https://ebird.org/checklist/S110096595. eBird: An online database of bird distribution and abundance [web application]. eBird, Ithaca, New York. Available: http://www.ebird.org. (Accessed: January 10, 2023).

Cañizares-Morera, Maikel (2022b). eBird Checklist: https://ebird.org/checklist/S100201334. eBird: An online database of bird distribution and abundance [web application]. eBird, Ithaca, New York. Available: http://www.ebird.org. (Accessed: January 10, 2023).

Carpenter, J. (2022). eBird Checklist: https://ebird.org/checklist/S120747444. eBird: An online database of bird distribution and abundance [web application]. eBird, Ithaca, New York. Available: http://www.ebird.org. (Accessed: January 10, 2023).

Catanach, T., R. H. Matthew, J. M. Allen, J. A. Johnson, R. Thorstrom, S. Palhano, C. P. Thunder, J. C. Gallardo & J. D. Weckstein (2021). Systematics and conservation of an endemic radiation of *Accipiter* hawks in the Caribbean islands, *Ornithology*, Volume 138, Issue 3, 1 July 2021, ukab041, https://doi.org/10.1093/ornithology/ukab041

Chambon, R., G. Gélinaud, J. M. Paillisson (2019). The first winter influences lifetime wintering decisions in a partially migrant bird. *Animal Behaviour* 149, 23-32.

Chapman, B. B.; Ch. Brönmark, J. Nilsson & L. Hansson (2011). The ecology and evolution of partial migration. *Oikos* (120): 1764–1775. doi: 10.1111/j.1600-0706.2011.20131.x

Chesser, R, S. Billerman, K. Burns, C. Cicero, L. Dunn, B. Hernández-Baños, R. Jiménez, A. Kratter, N. Mason, P. Rasmussen, J. Remsen, D. Stotz and K. Winker (2022). Sixty-third supplement to the American Ornithological Society's Check-list of North American Birds. *Ornithology*. 139. 10.1093/ornithology/ukac020.

Clements, J. F., T. S. Schulenberg, M. J. Iliff, T. A. Fredericks, J. A. Gerbracht, D. Lepage, S. M. Billerman, B. L. Sullivan, and C. L. Wood. 2022. The eBird/Clements checklist of Birds of the World: v2022. Downloaded from https://www.birds.cornell.edu/clementschecklist/download/

Correa, P. (2022). eBird Checklist: https://macaulaylibrary.org/asset/463466771. eBird: An online database of bird distribution and abundance [web application]. eBird, Ithaca, New York. Available: http://www.ebird.org. (Accessed: January 10, 2023).

Cory, C.B. (1889). The Birds of the West Indies, including the Bahama Islands, the Greater and Lesser Antilles, excepting the islands of Tobago and Trinidad, *Auk* 3: 454-472.

d' Orbigny, A. in de la Sagra, R. (1839). *Historia física, política y natural de la isla de Cuba*; Segunda parte. Historia natural. Tomo III. Mamíferos y Aves. Libreria de Arthus Bertrand.

De Jong, M. J. (2020). Northern Rough-winged Swallow (*Stelgidopteryx serripennis*), version 1.0. In *Birds of the World* (A. F. Poole and F. B. Gill, Editors). Cornell Lab of Ornithology, Ithaca, NY, USA. https://doi.org/10.2173/bow.nrwswa.01

Dove, C.J. and Banks, R.C. (1999). A taxonomic study of Crested Caracaras (Falconidae). Wilson Bulletin. 111(3): 330–339.

eBird. 2021. eBird: An online database of bird distribution and abundance [important-changes-to-exotic-species-in-ebird]. eBird, Cornell Lab of Ornithology, Ithaca, New York. Available: http://www.ebird.org. (Accessed: November 19, 2022).

eBird. 2022a. eBird: An online database of bird distribution and abundance. 2022-ebird-taxonomy-update. eBird, Cornell Lab of Ornithology, Ithaca, New York. Available: http://www.ebird.org. (Accessed: November 19, 2022).

eBird. 2022b. eBird: An online database of bird distribution and abundance. ebird.org/map/blkvul. eBird, Cornell Lab of Ornithology, Ithaca, New York. Available: http://www.ebird.org. (Accessed: January 10, 2023).

eBird. 2022c. eBird: An online database of bird distribution and abundance. ebird.org/barchart/CU. eBird, Cornell Lab of Ornithology, Ithaca, New York. Available: http://www.ebird.org. (Accessed: January 10, 2023).

eBird. 2022d. eBird: An online database of bird distribution and abundance. ebird.org/map/relhon. eBird, Cornell Lab of Ornithology, Ithaca, New York. Available: http://www.ebird.org. (Accessed: January 10, 2023).

Eisenmann, E. (1962). Notes on nighthawks of the genus *Chordeiles* in southern Middle America, with a description of a new race of *Chordeiles minor* breeding in Panama. *American Museum Novitates* 2094:1-21.

Espin, M. E., and L. G. Rivera (2010). First breeding record of Black Swift *Cypseloides niger* in Cuba. *Cotinga* 32:146–147.

Fidler, W. (2018). eBird Checklist: https://ebird.org/checklist/S42278780. eBird: An online database of bird distribution and abundance [web application]. eBird, Ithaca, New York. Available: http://www.ebird.org. (Accessed: January 10, 2023).

Friedmann, H. (1950). The Birds of North and Middle America. Part XI. Cathartidae to Falconidae. U.S. *National Museum Bulletin* no. 50. Smithsonian Institution, Washington, D. C., USA.

Garrido, O. H. & F. García (1975). *Catálogo de las Aves de Cuba*. Academia de Ciencias de Cuba, La Habana.

Garrido, O. H. & G. Reynard (1998). Is the Greater Antillean Nightjar, *Caprimulgus cubanensis* (Aves: Caprimulgidae), a composite species? *Ornitología Neotropical* (9): 1–12.

Garrido, O. H. & H. González (1980). Nuevos reportes de aves para Cuba. *Miscelánea Zoológica* 9:4.

Garrido, O. H. & Kirkconnell, A. 1990b. La Tórtola *Streptopelia decaocto* (Aves: Columbidae) en Cuba. *El Pitirre*, 3(4): 2.

Garrido, O. H. (2001). A new subspecies of the Burrowing Owl *Speotyto cunicularia* in Cuba. Cotinga 15:75-78.

Garrido, O. H., & A. Kirkconnell (2000). *Aves de Cuba*. Cornell University Press, Ithaca, NY.

Garrido, O. H., & A. Kirkconnell (2011). *Aves de Cuba*. Cornell University Press, Ithaca, NY.

Garrido, O. H., & J. W. Wiley (2010). First Cuban Occurrence of Orange Bishop (*Euplectes franciscanus*). *Journal of Caribbean Ornithology* 23:55-57.

Garrido, O.H. (2001). Was Red-legged Honeycreeper *Cyanerpes cyaneus carneipes* in Cuba introduced from Mexico? *Cotinga* 15: 58.

Garrido, O.H. and García-Montaña, F. (1967). El "Arrocero Negrito" *Volatinia jacarina splendens* (Vieillot) (Fringilidae, Aves) en Cuba. Trabajo de Divulgación No. 50, Museo "Felipe Poey" Capitolio Nacional, Academia de Ciencias de Cuba.

Gerbracht, J. and A. Levesque (2019). *The Complete Checklist of the Birds of the West Indies: v1.0*. BirdsCaribbean Checklist Committee. www.birdscaribbean.org/caribbean-birds.

Gerbracht, J., and A. Levesque. (draft). The complete checklist of the birds of the West Indies: v2.0. BirdsCaribbean Checklist Committee. www.birdscaribbean.org/caribbean-birds/

Gles, L. (2022). eBird Checklist: https://ebird.org/checklist/S120870865. eBird: An online database of bird distribution and abundance [web application]. eBird, Ithaca, New York. Available: http://www.ebird.org. (Accessed: January 10, 2023).

González Alonso, H., L. Rodríguez Schettino, A. Rodríguez, C. A. Mancina e I. Ramos García. 2012. *Libro Rojo de los Vertebrados de Cuba*. Editorial Academia, La Habana.

González, H. & E. Pérez (2010). Sitios importantes para las aves migratorias en Cuba. In *Áreas Importantes para la Conservación de las Aves en Cuba*. Susana Aguilar (edt.). Editorial Academia: 26.

González, H. (1996). *Composición y abundancia de las comunidades de aves residentes y migratorias en Cuba occidental y central durante el período migratorio* (tesis en opción al título de doctor en ciencias). Instituto de Ecología y Sistemática, La Habana.

González, H., E. Pérez, P. Rodríguez & O. Barrio (2008). Composición y abundancia de las comunidades de aves terrestres residentes y migratorias en cayo Sabinal, Cuba. *Poeyana*. (496): 23-32.

González, H; E. Pérez, P. Rodríguez & O. Barrio (2005). Adiciones a la Avifauna Terrestre de Cayo Sabinal. *The Journal of Caribbean Ornithology*, 18 (1): 24-28.

Gonzalez, M.A. (2021). eBird Checklist: https://ebird.org/checklist/S94328148. eBird: An online database of bird distribution and abundance [web application]. eBird, Ithaca, New York. Available: http://www.ebird.org. (Accessed: January 10, 2023).

Grimes, S. A. 1953. The Ringed Dove, *Streptopelia risoria*, nesting in Florida. *Florida Naturalist* 26:191, 205.

Groskopf, J. (2022). eBird Checklist: https://ebird.org/checklist/S120657347. eBird: An online database of bird distribution and abundance [web application]. eBird, Ithaca, New York. Available: http://www.ebird.org. (Accessed: January 10, 2023).

Guerra, J. L. & M. Cañizares (2019). Registro y establecimiento de la Miná Común (*Acridotheres tristis*) (Passeriformes: Sturnidae) en la Habana, Cuba. *Poeyana* 509, 18- 21.

Guerra, J.L. (2022). eBird Checklist: https:// ebird.org/caribbean/checklist/S110924589. eBird: An online database of bird distribution and abundance [web application]. eBird, Ithaca, New York. Available: http://www.ebird.org. (Accessed: January 09, 2023).

Gundlach, J. C. (1873). Catálogo de las Aves cubanas. *Anales de la Sociedad española de Historia Natural*, Tomo Segundo, Madrid, Don S. de Uhagon, Tesorero, 81-191.

Gundlach, J.C. (1856). Beiträge zur Ornithologie Cuba's. Nach Witlheilungen des Reisenden an Hr. Bez. - Dir. Sezekorn in Cassel; von Letzterem zusammengestellt. *Journal für Ornituologie*. September, 23.

Gunn, C., P. E. Lowther, C. T. Collins, J. P. Beason, K. Potter, and M. Webb (2021). Black Swift (*Cypseloides niger*), version 2.0. In *Birds of the World* (S. M. Billerman and B. K. Keeney, Editors). Cornell Lab of Ornithology, Ithaca, NY, USA. https://doi.org/10.2173/bow.blkswi.02

Halim, M. (2022). eBird Checklist: https:// ebird.org/checklist/S112686215. eBird: An online database of bird distribution and abundance [web application]. eBird, Ithaca, New York. Available: http://www.ebird.org. (Accessed: January 10, 2023).

Hegemann, A, P. P. Marra, I. Tieleman (2015). Causes and Consequences of Partial Migration in a Passerine Bird. *The American Naturalist* 186: 4. DOI: 10.1086/682667.

Hellmayr, C. E., and B. Conover (1949). Catalogue of birds of the Americas and the adjacent islands. Vol. 13, Part I, No. 4: Cathartidae-Acciptridae-Pandionidae-Falconidae. Chicago: Zool. Series, Field Museum of Natural History.

Hernández-Peraza, C. (2023). eBird Checklist: https://ebird.org/checklist/S125528536. eBird: An online database of bird distribution and abundance [web application]. eBird, Ithaca, New York. Available: http://www.ebird.org. (Accessed: January 15, 2023).

Historical Records (1915). eBird Checklist: https://ebird.org/checklist/S124792350. eBird: An online database of bird distribution and abundance [web application]. eBird, Ithaca, New York. Available: http://www.ebird.org. (Accessed: January 10, 2023).

Historical Records (1949). eBird Checklist: https://ebird.org/checklist/S125851876. eBird: An online database of bird distribution and abundance [web application]. eBird, Ithaca, New York. Available: http://www.ebird.org. (Accessed: January 10, 2023).

Historical Records (1949). eBird Checklist: https://ebird.org/checklist/S125851876. eBird: An online database of bird distribution and abundance [web application]. eBird, Ithaca, New York. Available: http://www.ebird.org. (Accessed: January 10, 2023).

Historical Records (1963). eBird Checklist: https://ebird.org/checklist/S124313162. eBird: An online database of bird distribution and abundance [web application]. eBird, Ithaca, New York. Available: http://www.ebird.org. (Accessed: January 10, 2023).

Historical Records (1978). eBird Checklist: https://ebird.org/checklist/S124974946. eBird: An online database of bird distribution and abundance [web application]. eBird, Ithaca, New York. Available: http://www.ebird.org. (Accessed: January 10, 2023).

Historical Records (1985). eBird Checklist: https://ebird.org/checklist/S122568832. eBird: An online database of bird distribution and abundance [web application]. eBird, Ithaca, New York. Available: http://www.ebird.org. (Accessed: January 10, 2023).

Historical Records (1987). eBird Checklist: https://ebird.org/checklist/S122959716. eBird: An online database of bird distribution and abundance [web application]. eBird, Ithaca, New York. Available: http://www.ebird.org. (Accessed: January 10, 2023).

IUCN (2000): http.//www.iucn.org. Guidelines for the prevention of biodiversity loss caused by alien invasive species.

IUCN Standards and Petitions Committee (2019). *Guidelines for Using the IUCN Red List Categories and Criteria*. Version 14. Prepared by the Standards and Petitions Committee. Downloadable from http://www.iucnredlist.org/documents/RedListGuidelines.pdf

Jovel, R. (2020). eBird Checklist: https://macaulaylibrary.org/asset/248669921. eBird: An online database of bird distribution and abundance [web application]. eBird, Ithaca, New York. Available: http://www.ebird.org. (Accessed: January 10, 2023).

Jovel, R. (2022). eBird Checklist: https://macaulaylibrary.org/asset/456494571. eBird: An online database of bird distribution and abundance [web application]. eBird, Ithaca, New York. Available: http://www.ebird.org. (Accessed: January 10, 2023).

Kirkconnell P., A., D. F. Stotz, and J. M. Shopland, eds. 2005. Cuba: Península de Zapata. *Rapid Biological Inventories Report 07*. The Field Museum, Chicago.

Kirkconnell, A., G. M. Kirwan, O. H. Garrido, A. D. Mitchell & J. W. Wiley (2020). *The Birds of Cuba, an Annotated Checklist*. BOU Checklist 26. British Ornithologists' Club, Tring.

Kirwan, G. M. (2000). Rose-ringed Parakeet (*Psittacula krameri*) Recorded in the West Indies. *El Pitirre*, vol. 13 No. 2.

Kirwan, G. M., A. Levesque, M. Overle & C. J. Sharpe (2019). *Birds of the West Indies*. Lynx Editions.

Kirwan, G. M., R. O. Bierregaard, H. F. Greeney, J. del Hoyo, N. Collar, J. S. Marks, and C. J. Sharpe (2022). Cuban Kite (*Chondrohierax wilsonii*), version 1.0. In *Birds of the World* (B. K. Keeney, Editor). Cornell Lab of Ornithology, Ithaca, NY, USA. https://doi.org/10.2173/bow.hobkit2.01

Lack, D. (1943). The problem of partial migration. *Br. Birds* 37: 122–130.

Lembeye, J. (1850). *Aves de la isla de Cuba*, Imprenta del Tiempo, La Habana.

Lewis, A. (2009). eBird Checklist: https:// ebird.org/checklist/S20771219. eBird: An online database of bird distribution and abundance [web application]. eBird, Ithaca, New York. Available: http://www.ebird.org. (Accessed: January 10, 2023).

Llanes, A., E. Pérez Mena, H. González Alonso, A. Pérez Hernández and P. Rodríguez Casariego (2016). Nuevos Registros de Aves para la Península de Guanahacabibes, que Incluyen el Primer Registro de *Cardellina pusilla pileolata* para Cuba. *Poeyana* 502:63-71.

Lockett, R. (2022). eBird Checklist: https://ebird.org/checklist/S107479598. eBird: An online database of bird distribution and abundance [web application]. eBird, Ithaca, New York. Available: http://www.ebird.org. (Accessed: September 18, 2022).

López del Castillo, S. (2022). eBird Checklist: ebird.org/checklist/S119324292. eBird: An online database of bird distribution and abundance [web application]. eBird, Ithaca, New York. Available: http://www.ebird.org. (Accessed: January 10, 2023).

López del Castillo, S., C. Hernández Peraza and R. López Silvero, *in press*. Segundo registro para Cuba de *Setophaga coronata auduboni* (Aves: Passeriformes: Parulidae).

Lundberg, P. (1988). The Evolution of Partial Migration in Birds. *Tree* 3: 7.

Mantilla, C. (2022). eBird Checklist: https://ebird.org/checklist/S118476405. eBird: An online database of bird distribution and abundance [web application]. eBird, Ithaca, New York. Available: http://www.ebird.org. (Accessed: January 10, 2023).

Marín, A. M., and J. E. Sánchez. (1998). Breeding of the Black Swift (*Cypseloides niger*) in Costa Rica. *Ornithologia Neotropical* 9:219-221.

Milan, L. (2022). eBird Checklist: https://ebird.org/checklist/S120445776. eBird: An online database of bird distribution and abundance [web application]. eBird, Ithaca, New York. Available: http://www.ebird.org. (Accessed: January 10, 2023).

Monroe, Burt Leavelle Jr, A Distributional Survey of the Birds of Honduras. (1965). LSU Historical Dissertations and Theses. 1046. https:/ /digitalcommons.lsu.edu/gradschool_disstheses/1046

Morrison, J. L. and J. F. Dwyer (2021). Crested Caracara (*Caracara plancus*), version 1.0. In *Birds of the World* (A. F. Poole, Editor). Cornell Lab of Ornithology, Ithaca, NY, USA. https://doi.org/10.2173/bow.y00678.01

Navarro y Fernández-Ordoñez (2017). First Record of Eurasian Blackcap (*Sylvia atricapilla*) for Cuba and the West Indies. in Navarro, N. & E. Reyes. *Annotated Checklist of the Birds of Cuba*. Ediciones Nuevos Mundos, St. Augustine, FL, No. 1.

Navarro, N. & E. Reyes (2017). *Annotated Checklist of the Birds of Cuba*. Ediciones Nuevos Mundos, St. Augustine, FL, No. 1.

Navarro, N. (2019). *Annotated Checklist of the Birds of Cuba 2018-2019*. Ediciones Nuevos Mundos, St. Augustine, FL, No. 2.

Navarro, N. (2020). *Annotated Checklist of the Birds of Cuba 2020*. Ediciones Nuevos Mundos, St. Augustine, FL, No. 3.

Navarro, N. (2022a). *Annotated Checklist of the Birds of Cuba 2021*. Ediciones Nuevos Mundos, St. Augustine, FL, No. 5.

Navarro, N. (2022b). eBird Checklist: https://ebird.org/caribbean/checklist/S114044711. eBird: An online database of bird distribution and abundance [web application]. eBird, Ithaca, New York. Available: http://www.ebird.org. (Accessed: January 10, 2023).

Navarro, N. (2022c). eBird Checklist: https://ebird.org/checklist/S124254372. eBird: An online database of bird distribution and abundance [web application]. eBird, Ithaca, New York. Available: http://www.ebird.org. (Accessed: January 10, 2023).

Navarro, N. (2022d). eBird Checklist: https:// ebird.org/checklist/S124635819. eBird: An online database of bird distribution and abundance [web application]. eBird, Ithaca, New York. Available: http://www.ebird.org. (Accessed: January 10, 2023).

Navarro, N. (2022e). eBird Checklist: https://ebird.org/checklist/S124696955. eBird: An online database of bird distribution and abundance [web application]. eBird, Ithaca, New York. Available: http://www.ebird.org. (Accessed: January 10, 2023).

Navarro, N. (2022f). eBird Checklist: https://ebird.org/checklist/S116560711. eBird: An online database of bird distribution and abundance [web application]. eBird, Ithaca, New York. Available: http://www.ebird.org. (Accessed: January 10, 2023).

Newton, I. (2008). *Migration ecology of birds*. Academic Press.

Oberholser, H. C. (1912). The Status of *Butorides brunescens* (Lembeye). *Proceedings of the Biological Society of Washington* 25: 53-56.

Orihuela, J. (2019). Annotated List of Late Quaternary Extinct Birds of Cuba. *Ornitología Neotropical*, 30: 57-67.

Ortega-Piferrer, A. (1983). Reporte de Records Ornitológicos Capturados en Gibara. Trabajo de Divulgación No. 1. Museo de Historia Natural Joaquín de la Vara, Sectorial de Cultura, Gibara, Holguín.

Plasencia, C.L., Padilla, M., Segovia, Y. Viña, N. and Rodríguez, F. (2019). Reporte de la Bijirita de Connecticut (*Oporornis agilis*, Aves: Parulidae) en el Oriente de Cuba. *Novit. Caribaea* 14: 163-166.

Polan, R. (2022a). eBird Checklist: https://ebird.org/checklist/S107937907. eBird: An online database of bird distribution and abundance [web application]. eBird, Ithaca, New York. Available: http://www.ebird.org. (Accessed: January 10, 2023).

Polan, R. (2022b). eBird Checklist: https://ebird.org/checklist/S111895548. eBird: An online database of bird distribution and abundance [web application]. eBird, Ithaca, New York. Available: http://www.ebird.org. (Accessed: January 10, 2023).

Purdy, B. (2009). eBird Checklist: https://ebird.org/checklist/S7520449. eBird: An online database of bird distribution and abundance [web application]. eBird, Ithaca, New York. Available: http://www.ebird.org. (Accessed: January 10, 2023).

Pyle, P. & DeSante, D. F. (2003). Four-letter and Six-letter Alpha Codes for Birds Recorded from the American Ornithologists' Union Check-list Area. *North America Bird Bander*, (28): 64-79.

Pyle, P. (1997). *Identification Guide to North American birds*. Vol. 1. Slate Creek Press, Bolinas, California.

Raffaele, H., J. W. Wiley, O. H. Garrido, A. Keith & J. Raffaele (1998). *A Guide to the Birds of the West Indies*. Princeton Univ. Press, Princeton, NJ.

Ragues, P. V. (1914). Museo cubano "Gundlach", Catálogo general. Instituto de Segunda Enseñanza de la Habana. Imprenta Cuba Intelectual, Habana, Santo Tomás 30, Cerro.

RARC, Registro de Aves Raras en Cuba (2021). eBird Checklist: https:// ebird.org/checklist/S122553242. eBird: An online database of bird distribution and abundance [web application]. eBird, Ithaca, New York. Available: http://www.ebird.org. (Accessed: January 10, 2023).

RARC, Registro de Aves Raras en Cuba (2022a). eBird Checklist: https:// ebird.org/checklist/S122569666. eBird: An online database of bird distribution and abundance [web application]. eBird, Ithaca, New York. Available: http://www.ebird.org. (Accessed: January 09, 2023).

RARC, Registro de Aves Raras en Cuba (2022b). eBird Checklist: https:// ebird.org/checklist/S122560689. eBird: An online database of bird distribution and abundance [web application]. eBird, Ithaca, New York. Available: http://www.ebird.org. (Accessed: January 09, 2023).

RARC, Registro de Aves Raras en Cuba (2022c). eBird Checklist: https:// ebird.org/checklist/S122559926. eBird: An online database of bird distribution and abundance [web application]. eBird, Ithaca, New York. Available: http://www.ebird.org. (Accessed: January 09, 2023).

RARC, Registro de Aves Raras en Cuba (2022d). eBird Checklist: https://ebird.org/checklist/S122784724. eBird: An online database of bird distribution and abundance [web application]. eBird, Ithaca, New York. Available: http://www.ebird.org. (Accessed: January 10, 2023).

Robson, C. (2022). eBird Checklist: https://ebird.org/checklist/S105434124. eBird: An online database of bird distribution and abundance [web application]. eBird, Ithaca, New York. Available: http://www.ebird.org. (Accessed: September 18, 2022).

Rodríguez Castaneda, Y., J.W. Wiley, and O.H. Garrido, 2017. Additional records of Lazuli Bunting (*Passerina amoena*) and first records of several wild-caught exotic birds for Cuba. *The Journal of Caribbean Ornithology*, Vol. 30(2):134–142.

Rodríguez, D., E. Ruiz, A. Parada, A. Hernández (2014). Aves (p. 218-310) in Rodríguez, D.; Arias, A.; Ruiz, E. eds. (2014). *Fauna Terrestre del Archipiélago Sabana-Camagüey, Cuba*. Editorial Academia, La Habana.

Rodríguez, Y., O. H. Garrido, J. W. Wiley & A. Kirkconnell (2005). The Common Kingfisher (*Alcedo atthis*): An Exceptional First Record for the West Indies and the Western Hemisphere. *Ornitología Neotropical* 16: 141.

Rodríguez-Castañeda, Y. (2022). eBird Checklist: https://ebird.org/caribbean/checklist/S106136763. eBird: An online database of bird distribution and abundance [web application]. eBird, Ithaca, New York. Available: http://www.ebird.org. (Accessed: January 10, 2023).

Romagosa, C. M. and S. G. Mlodinow (2022). Eurasian Collared-Dove (*Streptopelia decaocto*), version 1.1. In *Birds of the World* (P. Pyle, P. G. Rodewald, and S. M. Billerman, Editors). Cornell Lab of Ornithology, Ithaca, NY, USA. https://doi.org/10.2173/bow.eucdov.01.1

Romagosa, C. M., and R. F. Labisky (2000). Establishment and dispersal of the Eurasian Collared-Dove in Florida. *Journal of Field Ornithology* 71(1):159–166.

Ruiz, E., A. Árias, D. Rodríguez, P. Blanco, P. Rodríguez, E. Pérez, A. Llanes, H. González, B. Sánchez & A. Parada (2009). Avifauna de los cayos Santa María, Ensenachos y Las Brujas, noreste de Villa Clara, Cuba. *Mesoamericana 13*(1): 44-55.

Ruiz, E., A. Arias, R. Arias, M. Triana, Y. Garcia, D. Martín, D. M. Aguilera y F. R. Rodríguez (en prensa). Connecticut Warbler (*Oporornis agilis*) and other Interesting Sightings for Santa María key, Sabana - Camagüey Archipelago, Cuba.

Ryall, C. (2016). Further records and updates of range expansion in House Crow *Corvus splendens*. *Bull. B.O.C.* 136 (1).

Selander, R. K. 1954. A systematic review of the booming Nighthawks of western North America. *Condor*, vol. 56, pp. 57-82.

Smith, P. W. (1987). The Eurasian Collared-Dove arrives in the Americas. *American Birds* 41(5):1370–1379.

Suárez, W. (2022). Catalogue of Cuban fossil and subfossil birds. Bulletin of the British Ornithologists' Club, 142(1): 10-74. doi.org/10.25226/bboc.v142i1.2022.a3.

Syzdek, D. (2022). eBird Checklist: https://macaulaylibrary.org/asset/469108701. eBird: An online database of bird distribution and abundance [web application]. eBird, Ithaca, New York.

Vega, J.C. (2022). eBird Checklist: https://ebird.org/caribbean/checklist/S102635064. eBird: An online database of bird distribution and abundance [web application]. eBird, Ithaca, New York. Available: http://www.ebird.org. (Accessed: January 10, 2023).

Verdecia-Díaz, M. (2021). eBird Checklist: https://ebird.org/caribbean/checklist/S94181777. eBird: An online database of bird distribution and abundance [web application]. eBird, Ithaca, New York. Available: http://www.ebird.org. (Accessed: January 10, 2023).

Vigors, N. A. 1827. XLVI. Sketches in Ornithology, &c. &c. [Continued from p. 246.] On some species of Birds from Cuba. *Zoological Journal*, London 3 p.434.

Wotzkow, C. (1991). New subspecies of Gundlach's Hawk, *Accipiter gundlachi*. Pp. 271–281 in: Chancellor & Meyburg (1991).

Zúñiga, D. S. (2016). *On the ecology and evolution of partial migration: a field study on migrant and resident European blackbirds* (Dissertation submitted for the degree of Doctor of Natural Sciences. Universität Konstanz, Faculty of Sciences, Department of Biology.

Made in United States
Orlando, FL
02 December 2023